Leading
Turnaround
Churches

By Gene Wood

ChurchSmart
RESOURCES

St. Charles, IL 60174
1-800-253-4276

Published by ChurchSmart Resources

We are an evangelical Christian publisher committed to producing excellent products at affordable prices to help church leaders accomplish effective ministry in the areas of Church planting, Church growth, Church renewal and Leadership development.

For a free catalog of our resources call 1-800-253-4276.

Cover design by: Julie Becker

Manuscript edited by: Kim Miller

© copyright 2001
  by Gene Wood

ISBN#: 1-889638-21-8

Leading
Turnaround
Churches

CONTENTS

FOREWORD

I would like to heartily endorse this book by Dr. Gene Wood. I have known Gene personally for a time, and he is extremely qualified to write such a book. Two qualities I appreciate so much about Gene's leadership are his success in the pastorate which has turned around a number of struggling churches and his practical and pragmatic solutions for today's turnaround churches.

I know of no one in church pastoral ministries who is more qualified to speak to issues specifically related to church leadership than Gene Wood. I hope that you will take this opportunity to make the insights which Gene has shared in these pages available to many pastors and church leaders. I'm confident this material will be helpful and encouraging to many leaders in turnaround situations. May it serve you well!

Sincerely,

Hans W. Finzel, D.Miss
Executive Director, CBI

INTRODUCTION

Yes you can!

The fact you have purchased this manual on Turnaround Leadership is a strong indication you can be used of God to lead turnaround in your local church. You have not given up. Possibly you've been beaten down. But you've made it back to your feet and are determined to grow and learn from your experiences. You are not content with the status quo. You feel called to the place of ministry you serve and are not ready to call it quits.

Perhaps your board questions your ability. Do you sense your denominational leaders have given up on you? Do seminars and pastor's conferences cause you to feel defeated, embarrassed, and lonely? Is your spouse the only one in your life who still believes you can overcome all obstacles and be an instrument for positive change? Nonetheless, there is hope. Yes, for you and your church.

Look up the word "average" and you'll find my picture

Chances are we have not met. There is a reason for that. I'm not famous. I'm a pastor like you. For the past 10 years I've served a church in Glendora, California.

This is the reason I know there is hope for you. I'm average. I'm average in appearance. I'm five feet nine inches, and shrinking slowly at age forty-eight. I go to the gym with some regularity, but that does not disguise the six pillows covering my abdominal six-pack. My face is showing age spots and my hairline is receding.

In high school I wrestled and participated in gymnastics. If you were to visit my alma mater in Auburn, Washington, you would search in vain for my name in the trophy case. I set no records. Left no legacy. Today I enjoy racquetball and played basketball until last year when I began to embarrass myself shamelessly. You see, I'm just average athletically.

I graduated from seminary in 1980. I'm grateful for my training, but I received no awards or scholarships. I doubt if many of my professors could put my name with a face. I was just average academically.

Since seminary in 1980, the Lord has not called me to be a church planter or to pastor churches in rapid population growth areas. Each of the churches I have pastored had long histories. One was over 100 years old. The churches that called me were average.

It probably comes as no surprise my pastoral abilities are average as well. Western Baptist College did present me with a preaching award. But it was a small school and, as I recall, not many men participated in the preaching contest that year. I don't manuscript my messages so any clever turn of a phrase or homiletic masterpiece is more coincidence than genius. Each weekend I preach three times. By the final delivery, I feel I've come close to communicating what I originally intended. By then, however, it's time to place the sermon notes in a file, and begin preparation for the next week. While I work hard at communicating God's Word with relevance, accuracy, and passion, my skills will never compare favorably to those pastors who broadcast their sermons weekly to a national audience.

How is this encouraging you may ask?

If your aspiration is to become one of the great religious leaders of our time, I probably cannot help you much. On the other hand, if you identify with being average, but have a deep unquenchable passion to be an effective turnaround leader, be encouraged. God often utilizes average people with an unusual determination in an extraordinary manner. One of my favorite passages says it this way:

> For consider your calling brethren, that there were not many
> wise according to the flesh, not many mighty, not many
> noble; but God has chosen the foolish things of the world
> to shame the wise, and God has chosen the weak things of
> the world to shame the things which are strong, and the base
> things of the world and the despised, God has chosen, the

things that are not, that he might nullify the things that are, that no man should boast before God (1 Corinthians 1:26-29 NASB).

What that says to me is the power for ministry is found in God and His Word. Since that is true, there is absolutely no difficulty from God's perspective in using average men and women who are committed to serving him in an attitude of self-denial.

While I have no illusions concerning my natural abilities, I have experienced the Lord's hand upon my life for turnaround ministry. God can and does choose to use average people to breathe fresh life into stagnant and even dying churches.

Looking for an easy fix? If so, you have the wrong book. Searching for practical and specific steps for small wins? Keep reading!

The degree of growth you will experience with these principles may be small or massive. That is up to you, your leadership team, and God. But I'm confident in assuring you that rigorous and prayerful application of the principles shared will bring change in your church. Turnaround always demands change. The church can either change their leader or its leader can decide to change.

This book is written with the surgeon-pastor in mind. Some of what is shared will be hard words. Turnaround is not for the faint of heart. I recommend you (pastor) read this book alone.

Envision this product as a tool kit. Pick and choose according to what is most helpful in your unique situation. It is probably unwise to use everything you'll read and hear. Be discreet (see chapter 8). A surgeon selects his instruments based upon the demands of the operation being performed. No two are identical.

The lessons shared in this book are passed along to give you confidence. Confidence is developed through winning experiences, successes and achievement.

You need confidence not more criticism

Pastors are magnets for criticism. They are called to confront sin. They must bring change. They offer advice and counsel. They are expected to be non-retaliatory. If they strike back or even defend themselves, there is a heavy price to pay. Pastors appear strong. People pay his salary so assume he works for them.

I would also add, many churches set up a form of congregational polity which encourages outspoken criticism in a public setting. The pastor is to sit quietly while his personal finances and professional competency are openly debated.

I assume you, pastor friend, have had all the critiquing needed. How about some proactive and helpful suggestions? This is the heart of this book.

You may also be suffering from burnout. I'm convinced burnout does not come from working hard. It is caused by working hard with few results. Can you identify with the following?

> We trained hard . . . but it seemed that every time we were beginning to form up teams we would be reorganized . . . I was to learn later in life that we tend to meet any new situation by reorganizing; and a wonderful method it can be for creating the illusion of progress while producing confusion inefficiency and demoralization.

> —Petronius Arbiter (210 B.C.)

If you are sufficiently weary of restructuring and holding endless meetings only to do the same old thing, then this book is for you. After all, *if we always do what we've always done, we'll always get what we've always got.*

Can turnaround be guaranteed? No! I would be lying to tell you that. Are there risks? Yes! Am I confident these principles provide workable guidance for navigating the treacherous task of bringing life and vitality to your church? Yes—because I've seen them work!

If you're willing to outlive whatever is standing between your church's reality and effective ministry dreams, then you probably are better off approaching the suggestions of this book with caution. Your sense of urgency may not match the price you'll need to pay. On the other hand, if you are consumed by a sense of discontent with the present situation, there is help for you.

Is there really hope for me?

Yes, if you are fully committed to seeing positive change take place in your church and willing to pay the price. Yes, If you are convinced God has placed you in the church where you are, for the sake of winning the lost, building the saints, equipping the workers, and multiplying leaders.

Final note of caution

In ninth grade, Coach Shaw sent all of us out to the baseball field in our first period PE class for a distance run. I was feeling a little frisky and decided I wanted to win that day. Remember I was average. He pointed to a couple of backstops located off in the distance and instructed us to run from our location around both backstops and return to where we were.

Approximately half way I realized, to my amazement, I was running second. The only other boy with me was Dave McGinnis, our varsity runner. For once in my life I would finish first. One hundred yards from the finish line I sprinted. Dave didn't keep the pace. With renewed energy I gave my all. As I approached Coach Shaw, I heard his words of affirmation, "Good job, Wood. Just one more lap."

I don't remember how I placed that day, but it certainly was nowhere near first. I learned two valuable lessons: first, be clear on instructions before you take off; second, pacing is critical.

Turnaround is a worthy objective. It will not likely happen overnight. You should probably plan to invest at least seven years. It's a distance run not a sprint. Through these tools, I will be alongside you to coach you in the journey.

Yes you can!

CHAPTER 1

What Does a Turnaround Leader Look Like?

Predictable ceilings

Church growth literature has documented the predictable plateaus churches face. They are usually identified as an average worship attendance of 75, 200, 400, 800, and 1200 "caps." These caps, however, are elastic ceilings. You push over them and think all is smooth sailing only to discover a year later nothing has changed. The church's scope of ministry is approximately where it was twelve months previously. Frustrating to say the least. Methods, programs, and leadership style which worked so well in bringing the church to this size become less effective, even counterproductive. A church which has grown quickly, and seemingly effortlessly, suddenly reaches a brick wall. Now that momentum has been lost, turnaround is required. What type of leader can get the church growing again?

Confidence is critical

Effective turnaround leaders are not clones. They come in all sizes, shapes, personalities, and ages. What they share in common is self-confidence.

How does this square with what was said previously about being average? It is a mistake to confuse self-confidence with arrogance. Arrogant people don't feel a need for God. Self-confident church leaders are usually painfully aware of their personal weaknesses but have experienced the power of God working in and through them. They know the difference between natural talent and spiritual giftedness.

I was pleased to hear John MacArthur, pastor of the 10,000-member Grace Community Church in Panorama City, California, say he was not sure whether he would be able to repeat his story of growth in another place at another time. Rick Warren has admitted the same. This in no way mitigates their capabilities, nor is it false humility. And it certainly does not diminish their confidence that they are God's men in God's place doing God's work.

I bring these well-know names into the discussion to segue to a critical point. Whatever the turnaround leader looks like he probably will NOT look like John MacArthur, Rick Warren, Bill Hybels, Leith Anderson, or Charles Stanley. Turnaround leaders seldom mimic another leader. They learn all they can from them, then proceed to package their plans, styles, and timing to the situation in which they find themselves. What they do mirror, however, is the confidence of these great leaders.

Seldom do the mega-church pastors serve as the best models for those seeking to discover patterns and principles to guide them in turnaround. We need to look elsewhere.

Can a pastor do multiple turnarounds?

The answer is usually not. But sometimes.

George Barna in *Turnaround Churches*, Regal (1993) concluded that leaders who brought churches back from the brink were young, and seldom were able or willing to attempt to do so in more than one or two situations. He based his conclusions in the book upon interviews with 30 pastors. Since I happened to be one of those, I was obviously quite interested in his conclusions.

Even more disappointing to many, including myself, was his conclusion that what those pastors did could not be shared in a significantly helpful manner with others. He concluded that their "unique" gift mix and strengths, while observable, were probably not transferable!

> . . . a turnaround pastor is a truly unique human being, skilled in ways that are uncommon even among the ranks of the best-known and most talented clergy. Being a visionary leader is not, by itself, sufficient to prepare a person to lead a

dying church back to health ... it appears that relatively few leaders currently serving the church are truly turnaround pastors. And because of the enormous personal toll the turnaround process takes on people, even these individuals are likely to revive only one or two churches during their ministry careers. Thus, the chances of finding a turnaround pastor are slim. (p. 108–109)

While I admire Barna's research and literary skills, I simply differ.

Yes, the toll is terrific. I agree the skills necessary to direct a comeback are not synonymous with those of a church planter or the pastor who leads a steadily growing congregation.

No, I do not think turnaround pastors can only do it in one location. Part of their skill is assessing the needs of their particular congregations, the history of their churches, the cultures, the resources available, and then developing tailor-made strategies for their congregations. Neither do I believe the skills cannot be transferred. This book is written with the conviction they can be.

True turnaround pastors usually CAN do it again, and again, and again

One of my ministry heroes is Don Engram, who is currently shepherding the fast-growing flock of Palmcroft Baptist Church in Phoenix, Arizona. Don has effectively led four churches to significant growth in four states over four decades. He is now directing the efforts of this great church in a $6 million expansion project. Don is 70 years old. I believe he represents what can happen if pastors are lover-leaders, sensitive to the Holy Spirit. Good leaders change their styles to accommodate the needs, but the principles they've learned move with them from location to location.

The principles we consider are transferable to any pastor willing to grow and pay the price. Certainly some will have an advantage due to gifts, experience, upbringing, and personality. But if God has called us to a church, He does wish for it to be vital and spiritually alive. If you believe that, there is hope!

Turnaround leaders do not waste energy whining

I have long appreciated the wise writings of Fred Smith, Sr. He has helped me immensely through his writings. His words are tender yet ruthlessly practical. I met him for breakfast recently in preparation for this book. He was early (most superb leaders are). Apologizing for his casual attire, he explained his wife was now a semi-invalid; he had never had complete dexterity of his right hand, and had just undergone surgery on his left for carpel tunnel. He had to dress himself with neither hand able to button his shirt.

Before I could offer my sympathy he added, "Two words have become very important to me. They are *current reality*." He went on to explain that there is little value in spending energy worrying about what might be or should be. Leaders assess what is and go from there. Get on with it.

What is your current reality?

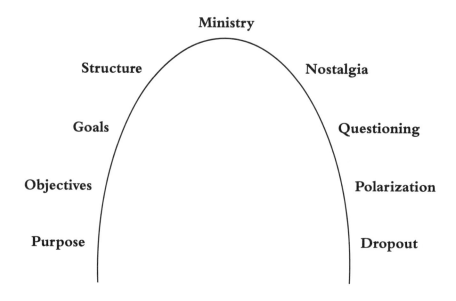

Where is your church on the bell curve? Have you crested? How many years has the curve continued downward? Denial gets us nowhere. Effective turnaround leaders sense the dynamics of Robert Dale's bell curve without ever having seen it.

Plateaued ministries will soon become dying institutions if they are not guided by turnaround leaders. What indicators might there be that a church is in danger? Three factors usually warn of impending decay:

1. Extreme and continued member dissatisfaction. When people's needs are not being met, problems lie ahead.

2. Low morale. When regular participants fail to see evidence of life (fruit bearing), they lose a heart for sacrifice and investment in the efforts of the church.

3. Declining or negative bottom lines. While numbers of worshipers, baptisms and dollars are not the sole criteria for gauging health, they are significant indicators.

While not as glaring as the above, a leader can look for more subtle diagnostic indicators. These might be viewed as signs of impending pathology. The main thing has been ignored for so long, the body is in danger of dying if:

1. The church consistently rewards activities unrelated to the main thing. This might be increasing the support of missionaries who do not fulfill your purpose statement, or placing people into positions of leadership who evidence no commitment to what your church purpose statement claims to uphold as important.

2. Activities do not follow purpose. The more programs the better, or so it seems. Yet, in many cases, these programs, which drain the church budget of thousands of dollars and demand thousands of man-hours, do little to produce fruit. Despite the fact that these programs do not produce character or conversions, they continue year after year. Numerous sacred cow programs are a sure sign a church is in trouble.

   This might be referred to as corporate cognitive dissonance. The cognitive dissonance theory assumes humans are cognitive beings. That is, what they believe must match what they do or one of three results will be forthcoming. One, they will change their behavior. Two, they will alter their beliefs. Or, three, they will go crazy.

   In the church the purpose statement (the main thing) expresses the core values. The programs are what they actually do. When the two do not line up, a form of schizophrenia develops and the congregation becomes dysfunctional.

3. The phantom limb complex exists. Individuals who have a limb amputated may still feel pain in that absent limb, or reach to scratch it. The automatic nervous system is causing them to respond through habit to non-existing needs. Is your church still holding services which meet no one's needs? Is your church practicing evangelistic methods which reach few? Are you insisting on a music style totally irrelevant to the community which you are desiring to touch?

4. There is evidence of a dead man walking. Does the church appear to have much motion without any awareness of purpose or plan? Three questions need to be asked. Can workers in the church articulate the main thing? Do workers understand how what they do contributes to the main thing? Do workers feel freedom to make adjustments to contribute better to the main thing?

Turnaround leaders understand the problems described above. When their church is dying, they sense it and long to do something to prevent further decline. This book will give practical suggestions to help turnaround leaders in assessment and corrective applications.

Must a church be large to be healthy?

Smaller churches can be healthy. Large churches can be sick. A few pastors are uncomfortable talking about change because they fear a knee-jerk reaction from laypeople afraid of becoming a mega-church. They can relax. Few need worry about becoming a mega-church. Of the 350,000 Protestant congregations in the United States:

Half average fewer than 75 at their principal weekly worship service

Three quarters average fewer than 150

Fewer than 5 percent average more than 350

Fewer than 1 percent average over 1000

Size really is not the issue for a turnaround leader. The focus should be health, not size. At age 49, I am not even interested in growing physically in size. I am more concerned than ever before about my overall health. While we cannot point to only one measurable factor to determine the health of a church—any more than a doctor can measure his patient's health by just one variable—as caregivers of the church we do need to take its pulse and see if it is fulfilling its Great Commission purpose. Dann Spader, founder of Sonlife, encourages pastors to consider the 10 percent rule. That is for every 10 people in Sunday morning worship at least one should be brought to faith that year. Thus, if your church averages 250 on Sunday morning you should expect to see at least 25 professions of faith or baptisms.

I think God loves small churches. Abraham Lincoln observed, "God must have loved the common man, He made so many of us." I suspect the same is true for the smaller and medium-sized church.

The issue is not size. What matters is how badly you wish to see your church become all God wishes for it to be!

Pastor friend, unless you have a burning desire to see it happen it won't! It's that simple. The role of the pastor has changed from the 1960s. At that time a congregation's expectations centered around the pastor's preaching and pastoral care. "Today the senior pastor must be focused on being proactive in leadership, vision casting and centered on mission." (**NetFax**, *Helping Church Leaders Make the Transition from the Present to the Future*, Number 80, September 15, 1997).

A turnaround pastor must be passionate about the need for radical change in his church. Cutting-edge churches have different styles and looks, but their senior pastors all share one common characteristic: big tears spring to their eyes for the lost."

A leader must have the heart of Jesus. The "want-to" comes before the "how-to."

Does it matter to you that people around you are lost? Jesus came "to seek and save the lost." He understood that as the central purpose of His life upon earth. By accomplishing His great redemptive plan He brought glory to the Father as nothing else could have done.

A turnaround leader might apply all the correct principles and practices without seeing the church grow (not likely, but possible). Successful turnaround leaders, however, refuse to allow their church to focus on secondary issues. They steadfastly resist playing church. They are not as worried about keeping their job as they are hearing the Lord say, "Well done, good and faithful servant."

The willingness to make tough decisions carries the risk of pain. Michael Jesen of Harvard University studied leadership traits that bring executives and their companies the greatest success. His surprising conclusion was that they understand "pain is good."

Average leaders assume corporate comfort is to be preferred. They operate under what he calls the Pain Avoidance Model (PAM). When the brain receives a negative report, or statistic, it chooses not to register it, and thus not to deal with it, when possible.

Effective leaders teach themselves to face up to the painful stimuli, and recognize what must be done and act (reported in Leadership Strategies Premier issue, p.8 — source was Geoffrey Colvin, Fortune Magazine).

What about those who say turnaround is nearly impossible?

As mentioned earlier, I had a personal interest in the conclusions drawn by George Barna in his 1993 book on this subject of turnaround. It was among the first to address the subject and for that we must all be grateful. However, I believe he drew some erroneous conclusions. He concludes, "While the chances are slim that a declining church can be turned around (p.6)."

Even more disconcerting for the 350,000 pastors in our country is his claim: "To turn around a church, a new pastor must be brought in to lead the revolution. Some churches probably have come back from the edge of extinction without a change in pastor. However, we did not find such a church." (p.47)

Aubrey Malphurs quotes Lyle Schaller and Ralph Neighbor Jr. as saying turnarounds cannot be done and/or little is known that will work (Vision America).

I believe Barna and others are wrong. At the risk of offending, there is a certain amount of ego posturing not taken into account by Barna's research and other similar studies.

Pastors often enjoy deflating the accomplishments of their predecessors and inflating their own accomplishments. Most every pastor I've known has considered himself to be walking into a turnaround situation. Few are willing to admit "My predecessor did such a great job of laying a foundation that growing this church is like falling off a log."

Furthermore, it is a well-known fact that a pastor's most effective ministry frequently does not begin until he has been at a church seven years. How does this reality fit with Barna's conclusion that a pastor must see immediate turnaround or be forever without hope?

In a long pastorate, a church is likely to go through several cycles of plateau, stagnation, and renewed vigor and growth. Womack, in his somewhat dated but nonetheless outstanding book *The Pyramid Principle of Church Growth* (Minneapolis: Bethany Fellowship, Inc., 1977) suggests churches are much like the physical bodies of children. The bone structure must be solidified to accommodate the next spurt of growth.

I have been amazed that few have stepped forward to challenge the conclusion that only new pastors can lead a church in effective turnaround. This is manifestly untrue and is circular reasoning. It begins by defining a "turnaround pastor" as one who brings about almost immediate growth to a declining church. Given that definition only a new pastor could qualify.

Recently a number of well-known mega-churches have admitted their attendance has declined for two or more years. Should we assume the only solution is for them to dismiss their excellent leaders?

I think not. The growth may never be as rapid as it was at one point, but my guess is that these competent leaders will figure out a way to turn the decline around and begin growing once again.

A pastor determined to bring about new life in his ministry must, however, be willing to change. Either the church must change its pastor or the pastor must change.

Over a period of 25 years, I've watched with fascination as some pastors have chosen to be voted out of their churches, leave the ministry, or hold a funeral service for their churches rather than change. Why? Is it too painful to admit what they're doing is not working? How can leaders expect their congregations to change if they themselves are unwilling to lead the way?

Turnaround will probably be a little bloodier for a pastor who has been serving in a church for several years than it would have been had he begun the process immediately. But it can be done. Speaking of blood, it is virtually impossible to perform surgery without blood being spilled. Turnaround leaders view themselves as surgeons, not butchers. They know the end result will not only bring glory to God, but good to the people they shepherd.

Summary

There are predictable numeric barriers at which progress stops in most congregations. Once the momentum is lost, a turnaround is required. Turnaround leaders come in all shapes, personalities, and sizes but they are all confident of their calling and have discovered transferable principles which permit them to participate in the miracle of turnaround more than once if required. These principles are best learned from those who have been gifted and called to this particular type of ministry rather than the typical mega-church pastor.

The bell curve is a simple tool to help ascertain how critical the condition of a church is. Once a pastor recognizes where his church is on this curve, he can decide which principles presented in later chapters should be applied.

No church is too small to accept the challenge of regaining vitality and health. God loves small churches too. What is required for any size church, however, is a leader with a fire in his gut for redemption of lost souls. This passion will likely be what sustains him in the heat of the spiritual battle. There is no turnaround without pain. The godly leader, therefore, accepts the role of a surgeon. The body of Christ must be made well.

CHAPTER 2

Is Faithfulness Enough?

I sat on the deck one cool Midwest morning watching my 12-year-old son on his maiden voyage commandeering the riding lawn mower. He was attempting to follow my detailed instructions. Tony watched carefully for rocks and made sure the tire marks in the grass overlapped six inches each time he circled. Around he went on the half-acre track. He made two full laps before stopping the mower and glancing sheepishly up to where I sat. He was doing everything perfectly, but he had neglected to engage the mower blade.

This incident reminds me of many churches I have observed over the years. They are busy, but having no impact. The purpose of the mower is to harvest grass. The purpose of God's church is to harvest people.

"Let a man regard us in this manner, as servants of Christ, and stewards of the mysteries of God. In this case, moreover, it is required of stewards that one be found trustworthy" ('faithful' KJV) (1 Corinthians 4:1-2, NASB).

Based largely upon this verse, people often conclude that God does not call us to be successful, only faithful. Is faithfulness enough? I will answer in two ways. Yes and no.

No, if "faithful" is interpreted to mean simply showing up. Would you consider your car faithful if it only ran four days a week? Would you accept newspaper service which failed to deliver the paper to your home every other day? What if your refrigerator stopped cooling one day per month? How do you think your bank would perceive your faithfulness if you missed one mortgage payment each year? If a student sits in class and daydreams, the "F" he receives will not stand for faithful. Why then do we call a church faithful if it is not routinely and successfully fulfilling the commission given to it?

Jesus stated in unambiguous language He "came to seek and save the lost" (Luke 19:10; Matthew 18:11). It is equally clear that His purpose has been passed on to His church (Matthew 28:19-20; John 17:18).

Just holding church services is not pleasing to the head of the church. Churches that follow the example of Christ will never be content with driving the mower in circles. They wish to engage the blade of evangelism to secure a harvest of souls.

Yes, however, faithfulness is enough if properly defined by fruitfulness. A couple of hints are given in this regard in 1 Corinthians 4. The word "regard" means "to give account or to calculate." The term "steward" refers to a manager of an estate. The steward does not own anything, but rather is entrusted with great responsibility and accountability for what belongs to another. Every Christian and each church must be prepared to give detailed account for what steps they have taken towards fulfilling the task assigned them.

Elsewhere in the New Testament we are provided insight into specifically what we will be held accountable for.

It is God's desire that we bear fruit (John 15:1-5). Several levels of fruit bearing are outlined:

*minus fruit (2a)

*mere fruit (2b)

*more fruit (2c)

*much fruit (5)

It is unarguably clear fruit-bearing is expected (Luke 13:6-9; Colossians 1:10; Romans 7:4). It is equally clear our Father may judge us for non-productivity (Matthew 21:19,43).

Note also that what we are is evidenced by production not profession (Luke 6:43-46).

As we study the Bible we discover there are two types of fruit expected from God's church. First is righteous character (Galatians 5:22; Ephesians

5:8-9; Philippians 1:11; Hebrews 12:11; James 3:17-18). Second is the fruit of conversions (John 4:34-36; Romans 1:13; Philippians 1:22; 4:17; 1 Corinthians 16:15).

Many churches today balk at this latter suggestion. While preaching/teaching to build up the body, they do not wish to be held accountable for significant outreach and evangelism. But a study of the term "fruit" makes it evident it is used for both character and conversions. A church focused solely upon building up the saints is only 50 percent productive at best.

Why do some churches hesitate to accept their mandate of fruit production and take seriously the charge to be effectively involved in the harvest of souls? Louis Moore, a Southern Baptist journalist, made the following observation in his book *The Truth in Crisis*. This book details the conflict between conservatives in the SBC, who believe in inerrancy, and moderates who hold to a "limited inerrancy," that is, that the Bible is not totally accurate in all matters to which it speaks.

> In sum, conservative pastors are generally more aggressive, energetic, and evangelistic at the local level than moderates. The result is seen in baptisms. Moderates do not brag about low baptism to membership ratios. When the astounding differences are cited, they tend to give such excuses as 'We're not in the numbers game' or 'We're building a strong fellowship' or 'Our church is in a slow growth area.' Rarely will a moderate concede that preaching style, church programs and theology might be factors (page 19).

A high view of Scripture should lead us to take seriously our responsibility to be engaged in the harvest of souls. We can draw strength from God's promise to provide the power necessary to make this a reality (Matthew 28:18; Acts 1:8).

Faithfulness must always include fruitfulness somewhere in its definition. Fruitfulness carries with it some wonderful benefits. First, it provides a special anointing from the Holy Spirit (John 20:21-22; Acts 1:8). There is an obvious spiritual adrenaline apparent in harvesting churches. Second, it leads to the confidence that flows from entering into an intimate partnership with God (1 Corinthians 3:9; Hebrews 3:1-2). And third, it creates a contagious atmosphere of joy. The book of Philippians is filled with references to "gospel" and "joy." Paul writes from prison to say his days are filled with joy, because fruit is being produced even while he is in undesirable surroundings. There is no such thing as an unhappy evangelist.

The great cover up

One reason a church may seek to deny the call to fruitfulness is to cover up the lack of the same. Besides not pleasing the Lord of the church, it pays a terrific price over time. People in the pews eventually tire of the lack of fruit and drift to another church where harvest is evident.

Eugene Heimler, a Holocaust survivor, wrote of an experiment in which Jews who had been working in a prison facility were, without explanation, suddenly ordered to move sand from one end of the camp to the other, then back to its original location. This process was repeated over a period of weeks.

Many prisoners who had been able to cling to life even while performing more difficult labors for their hated captors went berserk and were shot by the guards. Others threw themselves into the electrified wire fence.

Humans were not created for purposeless existence. If the purpose of Sunday morning is to convince people to return Sunday night and the purpose of Sunday night to persuade them to return Wednesday night, people will quickly grow weary. Intuitively Christians know spiritual procreation is what their souls have been designed for. It is built into their spiritual DNA. They long to be in a place where evangelism is expected and experienced on a regular basis. Non-fruit bearing churches lose people to other places of worship where God is expected to work, and does.

Turnaround leaders expect fruit

Jason Turkes was a 17-year-old high school honor student who was close to his mother, his wheel-chair bound father and younger brother. Jason was an excellent swimmer and avid scuba diver. One Tuesday morning he left the house, intent on exploring an underground spring found in a cave not too far from his west-central Florida home. He planned to return home that evening to celebrate his mother's birthday with his family.

It appears he swam into the cave and became lost, panicked and became wedged in a narrow passageway. Unable to free himself, he managed to take off his yellow metal air tank. He then unsheathed his diving knife. Using the air tank as a writing pad and the knife as a pen, he wrote his last communications to the outside world. The words were to his family, "Dad, Mom, and Christian, I LOVE YOU!" Then Jason ran out of oxygen and drowned.

Question. What do you suppose the Turkes' family did with that air tank? Discard it? Sell it for scrap? I think not. My guess is, that should you go to their home, you will find it displayed in a prominent spot, as a perpetual reminder of what was on their son's mind in the closing moments of his life.

What have we done with the closing words of Christ, "But you shall receive power when the Holy Spirit has come upon you; and you shall be My witnesses . . ."? The command is accompanied by the power to accomplish it effectively.

One common trait of every turnaround leader is a passionate desire to see a lost world reached with the good news of Christ's saving sacrifice. Without this fire burning in the gut, all the suggestions and insights of this book will prove minimally helpful.

> **Are you consumed with producing fruit? Are you prepared to be accountable for both character and conversions? The way you answer this question is more critical than any of the other principles which follow. It is the one non-negotiable essential if God is going to use you to be a change agent in His church.**

A family story

Several years ago we left our church in Glendora following a Sunday evening service. We agreed to pick up a bite to eat before heading home. After some discussion, an executive decision was made to find some fried chicken. We arrived at the drive-up window of a well-known franchise and eventually a voice came on from the other end of the squawk box, "Good evening. May I help you?" "Yes," I responded, "We'll take a bucket of white meat." "I'm sorry, but we don't have any white meat," came the answer from the other end. "Okay, then I guess we'll take a bucket of dark meat." "I'm sorry, but we don't have any dark meat." I couldn't believe what I was hearing. I turned and looked incredulously towards my wife to see if she had heard what I thought I had just heard. She had. "In that case," I responded, "I guess we'll take five Big Macs."

There was a long pause, then the voice said, "You know we don't have hamburgers!" Somewhat exasperated, I inquired, "If you don't have any chicken, then what do you have?" He proceeded to inform me, "We have fries, onion rings, soft drinks, mashed potatoes and corn-on-the-cob."

This particular chicken franchise had all kinds of side orders, but they didn't have the main thing! My family didn't go there for side orders. We wanted chicken.

How like some churches. The owner of the church has placed them there to serve fruit, the fruit of character and converts. But all they have are side orders: music, support groups, libraries, children's programs, recreational activities, and more. But week after week goes by and seldom are lost people brought into the kingdom. They lack the main thing.

If your church suffers from side-order thinking and you are determined by God's enablement to correct that, then read on. The task will not be easy, but it can be done.

A final word about the "Main Thing"

Much has been said in recent years about the main thing. The expression is from an old German proverb which stated, "The main thing is to keep the main thing the main thing."

In any corporate entity the main thing is its purpose statement. At Grace Church of Glendora, where I have pastored for the past 10 years, our purpose statement reads: "We exist to glorify God by developing committed followers of Jesus Christ who attract others to Him." Whatever your church purpose statement may be, it must certainly include both the development of character and converts. It may be broader than that, but these two goals must be owned by any New Testament church. This is the main thing for a local church.

Summary

What drives effective turnaround leaders is a conviction that God has called them into the work of harvest. While there seem to be parts of the globe which are not ripe "unto harvest" that cannot be said of the United States. Leaders who change the church from maintenance to fruitfulness are out in front. Evangelism is the highest priority. These leaders understand that most churches have heard too much about evangelism and yet failed to see it evidenced as a normal life practice by their leaders. Are you prepared to lead the way and not simply talk about it? People will do what people see. What is the "main thing" in your church? Are you happy with this?

CHAPTER 3

Considering the Cost

> If anyone comes to Me, and does not hate his own father and mother and wife and children and brothers and sisters yes, and even his own life, he cannot be My disciple. Whoever does not carry his own cross and come after Me cannot be My disciple. For which one of you, when he wants to build a tower, does not first sit down and calculate the cost, to see if he has enough to complete it? — Luke 14:26-28

May I suggest you think long and hard about the above passage as it relates to the awesome task of becoming a turnaround leader? In fact, we might insert turnaround leader in place of disciple. Whatever else is required it does demand willingness to place our task above all else. If Jesus died for His church, why should we be surprised that He asks His followers to do likewise?

In the previous chapter we discovered Christ's expectation in ministry is faithfulness resulting in fruitfulness. No man can produce spiritual fruit. That is precisely the point. We are called to walk in obedient fellowship to such a degree He can produce fruit through us.

Three facts to be faced

I will present a number of statistics in the next few pages. I do so not to fill space nor necessarily tell you something you don't already know. It is absolutely essential that anyone planning a turnaround be forewarned. As you review these facts I ask you to keep one thing in mind. If pastoring a church were easy, then most anyone could do it successfully. It is not! What our country needs is a special breed of church leaders. Let's face it. The current approach is not working.

Fact #1:
The church in the United States is not effectively reaching its community.

Tom Clegg, author of *Lost in America* (Group Publishing) and a missionary with Church Resource Ministries, studied 26 different denominations and arrived at the following conclusions (as reported in Ron Cline's HCJB newsletter 9/9/98):

- In the past decade the communicant membership of all Protestant denominations has declined by 9.5 percent (4,498,242) while in the same period the national population has increased by 11.4 percent (24,153,000) (according to Charles Arn, Autumn, 96 ASCG Journal of Church Growth).

- We close 72.11 churches a week or 10.27 per day in America.

- As many as 85 percent of America's Protestant churches are plateaued or declining in membership.

- Of the 350,000 churches, some 60,000 report not a single convert in a year's time (Barna).

Dr Virgil Gulker, a denominational leader, observed, "I look at the 350,000 religious congregations in this country with an average membership of roughly 100 people each, and I think of what those 35 million Christians could accomplish. The potential is awesome. We have five times more churches than post offices and thirty-five times more churches than McDonald's restaurants."

Finally, Thom Rainer in his book, *The Bridger Generation* (Nashville: Broadman & Holman, 1997), points out that the church has grievously neglected the souls of the bridger generation, which includes those born between 1980-1994. This generation, which will rival the boomers in quantity, is largely unreached. The Billy Graham School of Missions and Church Growth estimates that only 3 percent of them have been Christianized. Add to this the well-known fact that 80 percent of all those who come to faith do so before the age of eighteen. We are in danger of losing an entire generation.

Fact #2:
Strong pastoral leadership is essential for a resurgence of healthy churches.

Everything rises and falls on leadership. No serious student of church growth argues the fact that the pastor is key. Without his vision and guidance a church may have moments of greatness but will quickly lapse into stagnation and decline. Among other things the leader must select and build the team. He imparts the vision. He presses for spiritual maturity. He is the source of encouragement and sanity when everyone around is losing their minds. He is looked to for the development of a strategic plan and above all else is the one who takes the first step forward when the appropriate moment to take risks arises.

Fact #3:
Pastors are crumbling like sandcastles on the beach.

- More than 1300 pastors each month are forcibly terminated without just cause.

- A church that has fired a pastor has a 70 percent chance of doing the same to the following pastor.

- Each month more than 1200 pastors leave the ministry due to stress, church related issues, family issues, or burnout.

- Sixty-seven percent of pastors' wives say they're dissatisfied with their marriage.

- Seventy-five percent of pastors spend less than one evening per week with spouse or friends.

- Clergy divorce has risen 65 percent in the last 20 years.

- Fifty percent of seminary graduates leave the ministry after five years.

- Seventy percent of pastors say they don't have someone they consider to be a close personal friend.

- Seventy-one percent of pastors say they're having personal financial problems.

- The burnout rate is at an all time high with only 50 percent of pastors completing their working years as a pastor.

- Thirty percent of pastors have been fired at least once.

Denial helps no one

This is why we have begun this chapter by reviewing the realities on the pastoral landscape.

I was raised in a pastor's home. I remember a meeting held in the living room of the parsonage during my fifth grade year. The man who led music for my father had decided to oust my father from his pastorate. Voices were raised. I overheard it from the bedroom. I grew up knowing not everyone loved the pastor.

When I was 30, my father spoke at my ordination service in my first pastorate following seminary. I don't recall what he preached on but I vividly remember his words whispered in my ear following the service. He said simply, "Gene you can't ever say you didn't know what you were getting into."

You must admire the candor of the dentist who told her patient before touching a nerve, "This may hurt a little bit, or you might feel like you were just kicked in the face by a mule."

I would be less than honest not to tell anyone intending to direct a turn-around endeavor that it will be painful. What I cannot predict is how painful.

Seminaries have not adequately prepared pastors up till now

Talbot Seminary recently received a sizable grant from the Lilly Endowment for its program to enhance its students' preparedness for pastoral ministry. In the excellent proposal they highlighted a number of recurring patterns which need to be addressed. The following represents a synopsis of their findings.

- Too many men and women are entering ministry with a set of expectations that do not match reality. Students leave seminary believing they have been "called to preach." That may be true, but preaching is a small part of the pastoral expectations.

- Seminary students lack experience in dealing with conflict.

- Most pastors lack a personal support system.

- Pastors are on call 24 hours a day.

- Pastors burn out in part because they have never learned to take time for personal and spiritual disciplines that nurture health and spiritual vitality.

- Shepherding the congregation means introducing and implementing change. Change brings conflict.

- Relationships between co-workers and the laity are complex and challenging. Little has been taught on this issue.

The purpose of summarizing these points is to reiterate their importance. These pastoral realities are finally receiving attention from training institutions such as Talbot.

Do you have the disposition, strength and energy for the task?

The following questions will help you determine if you are prepared to lead a turnaround church. Be honest with yourself. If you do not rate yourself highly in these areas, are you willing to improve?

1) *Do you normally avoid conflict at any cost?*

Pat Keifert, president of Church Innovations Institute, tells of a congregational study done at Emory University by Nancy Ammerman.

> **It concluded that every congregation that successfully adapted and flourished in a changing community had a substantial church fight. Those that chose to avoid conflict at all costs failed to flourish.** *No Exceptions.* **(Net Results, January 1996)**

We will be saying much about conflict. Turnaround pastors must win. Some react vehemently to any discussion of winning and losing in ministry. I suspect the reaction is due in part to their concept of pastor as "shepherd." The term conjures up metaphors of gentleness, passivity, and tenderness. I recommend that those holding to such attributes as the primary characteristics of shepherds quickly sign up for the next Holy Lands tour.

Shepherds of Biblical times lived and worked in parched, inhospitable, and dangerous environs. The occupation was not for the weak. Shepherds encountered harsh weather, rough terrain, and predators — all threatening the sheep entrusted to their care.

Loneliness was expected, since they spent many hours surrounded by nothing but sheep, thieves, and wild animals looking for lunch. Solitude was the norm.

Uncertainty was daily fare. A shepherd had to take his sheep wherever the water and grazing led him. He was to be a master of the elements, familiar with the landscape, alert to the unexpected, and prepared to fight — alone when necessary.

All the while the shepherd never heard a word of gratitude from those he carried, restored, fed and protected.

He, however, did not work for the sheep. He tended sheep for his father or master. He took great pride in presenting the lambs to the one to whom he gave account. After all it was his career, his calling, his stewardship. His greatest achievement was being able to report, "I have lost none you have given me."

2) *Do you have a high energy level? Does work energize or deplete you?*

Some personality types do not lend themselves to the role of turnaround shepherd.

The MMPI designates these as the Asthenic Personality, which is noted for its:

- ◆ Easy fatigability

- ◆ Low energy level

- ◆ Lack of enthusiasm

- ◆ Marked incapacity for enjoyment

- ◆ Over-sensitivity to stress (physical or emotional)

- ◆ Weakness

- Lack of passion

- Distance, lack of involvement

- Hedonistic tendencies

- Physical sickness, need for a caregiver

Most turnaround leaders are considered workaholics. That is not necessarily true; they likely play with the same abandonment with which they work. They are simply high-energy people.

I believe working between 55 and 70 hours per week is not unreasonable. I arrive at that calculation by the following logic. Most dedicated lay leaders in our churches work at least 50 hours per week in their employment. They then invest another 10 to 15 hours in serving the Lord for a total of 60 to 65 hours. Shouldn't the senior pastor work at least as hard as they?

More energy will be expended during the turnaround than will be required after it is achieved. If this is serious business, it requires total commitment on behalf of the point person. We are at war for the soul of the church.

3) *Are you in good physical shape?*

Failure to exercise consistently makes a person sluggish and weary. Weariness makes cowards out of most of us. Cowards are not courageous leaders. Balanced dietary habits provide the resources our bodies need to fight stress and keep alert. Alert people are unafraid to make decisions. Turnaround leaders must make key decisions wisely.

4) *How would you rate your family life on a scale of 1-10?*

Is your marriage strong? Do you love your wife to the extent Christ loves the church? If you have children, are you spending quality time with each of them? If I were to look at your calendar would I find blocks of time each week dedicated to them?

Many find it advantageous to work off a desk calendar. Divide each week into 21 sections (morning, afternoon, evening - seven days per week). How many blocks have been reserved for family? By using a desk calendar you can avoid making appointments on the spot. Do not carry it with you. Do not take it home. When someone requests your time, simply write it down and assure him you will get back to him as soon as you arrive at the office and can check your calendar. In this manner you make appointments without others looking over your shoulder. Family is priority. If we lose them we have lost the battle.

Are you making it to their ball games and performances? Does your wife have a date night?

After 25 years of ministry, I assure you it is unnecessary to abuse your family life for ministry. However, there are other things which may need to be put on the back burner while children are growing up. Recreation, excessive softball, television and the like will wait.

I love racquetball. As we began our first pastorate after leaving seminary, I fully intended to continue playing three or more times per week. We had three small children. One afternoon I was heading out the door with bag in hand and my wife asked, "Can we talk when you get home?" I knew by the tone it would be an interesting conversation. That night she asked a probing question, "Gene, would you like to be a really good racquetball player . . . or a father?" I understood. Today, we are blessed with three grown children. What little I gave up has been amply repaid. Now, my wife is hustling me out the door to the gym.

Working hard does not require sacrificing family on the altar of success. If family life is not in order our credibility will be severely hindered. Turnaround pastors need every ounce of authentic credibility they can bring to the table. Church members are not looking for lofty words. They will follow authentic leaders.

5) *Are you willing to continue growing?*

Just the fact that you have invested time in this book hints you are! There are at least four growth ladders turnaround leaders must climb in the process of lifetime learning.

The first is the *content ladder*. Richard A. Swenson's book, *Margin* (Colorado Springs: Navpress, 1992), explains that we are living in an unprecedented time of expanding knowledge. We are in the information age. Its impact will be as cataclysmic as the industrial age of days past. Church members do not desire a know-it-all pastor. They do wish to be led by someone who is continually updating his understanding of their world.

The second is the *competency ladder*. Skills admirable in a thirty year old are laughable in a fifty year old. Without personal development we become hopelessly outdated. Acting your age is commendable. Being stagnant and predictable is boring.

Our church offers four styles of worship services each weekend. I have made it a personal goal to adjust my delivery, dress, and communications approach accordingly. No one demands I do this. I wish to be stretched. Because one style of preaching proved effective 20 years ago is no comfort. The world is changing. I actually change clothes several times as well. Is this a suggestion for anyone else? Not necessarily. I have noticed, however, that how we dress does impact our presence and manner of communicating. We use PowerPoint™ in some services, not in others. I don't want to become dependent on it. PowerPoint adds a new dimension to sermon preparation. Who would have thought 20 years ago pastors would ask one another, "Who is your clicker?"

We recently added live video feed to some of our services. Now I must learn techniques for the camera. What is distracting? What annoys? What connects? I purposely choose to utilize various microphones: pulpit mike, handheld with cord, handheld wireless or lapel. Sometimes I stay behind a pulpit, glass lectern or music stand; other times I walk throughout the audience or simply move on the platform. We also experiment with creative ways to participate at the Lord's Table.

I force myself to do various types of preaching, including systematic theology, book studies, life stages, topical, expositional, or question and answer.

Sometimes I study at a stand-up desk. Other times I study at my desk. I continually add a variety of study tools from a new Advanced Greek Grammar to the latest "how to" book on church growth.

Staff counselors free me from that responsibility. But occasionally I accept counseling requests for the purpose of keeping skills sharp. The same goes for bereavement and hospital calls.

The point is simply that everyone needs to be intentional in regards to improving professional competency.

Are you a lifetime learner? Or are you satisfied with where you are now?

The third ladder is the *capacity ladder*. This refers to the level of leadership you may attain. There are leaders (all pastors), leaders of leaders (pastors of multiple staff churches), leaders of the leaders of leaders (denominational executives and churches over 1000, which are essentially minidenominations), and finally leaders of the leaders of the leaders of leaders (those extremely gifted men and women whose counsel is sought by multiple denominations).

Each of us is wise to heed the counsel "know thyself." Are you in over your head? Is the church which you're contemplating assuming responsibility for a turnaround more than you're gifted to handle? If so, better you recognize that before everyone else does.

The "Peter Principle" is real. People are often promoted one level beyond their capabilities.

There is no shame in acknowledging you're in over your head. Turn the reigns over to someone else, and trust God to lead you to a place more fitting.

The fourth is the *character ladder*. The key question to be asked here is whether you can trust yourself with more authority. Turnaround leaders, if successful, will be granted immense freedom by their churches. Unfortunately freedom and authority are often accompanied by limited accountability. It is up to the leader to develop his own systems of accountability.

But our focus is specific. We are talking of turnaround leaders. No leader is likely to be given more privilege and trust by his people than the pastor who is able to take a seriously declining church and give it life and hope. Why? Because few are able to do this, as George Barna points out in his book *Turnaround Churches* (Ventura: Regal Books, 1993). Breathing life back into a new church is a modern day resurrection. A leader who does this is probably the reason the majority of the congregation is there. He likely led many of them to Christ personally. He is a hero.

If you possess such capabilities you will succeed. When you do, the temptations for moral failure will be at their peak. Look inside your soul. Can you handle it?

Effective turnaround leaders will never be unemployed — they have developed rare, valuable skills. They have learned to deal with people in a paradoxical manner, firm yet tender, self-confident yet vulnerable, serious and humorous (serious about what they're doing, and humorous regarding themselves), prayerful yet bold, people and task oriented. They learn to adjust leadership style to fit the demand. This unpredictability in leadership style is one of their most intriguing features. The constant in their life is their focus and passion about seeing their church revitalized. Their zeal in this area is viewed by many to be obsessive.

The Spirit-filled leader, the leader who has climbed the character ladder, is broken before God and will be as humble at the end of the victorious process as he was at the beginning.

Can you handle success? The question sounds like a no-brainer, like asking, "Would you like to be a millionaire?" There is a similarity between the two questions. 1 Timothy 6:5-11 is an excellent passage for meditation. Both ministerial success and wealth have proven to be the precipices from which too many have fallen to their destruction.

6) *Do you have an intuitive grasp of "churchianity?"*

Dr. Dennis Baker, former general director for CBAmerica's 1200 churches, once remarked, "Pastor's children who go into ministry appear to have a head start on the rest of us, and few ever make up the ground." When I heard Dennis' comment I shrugged it off. Over time I've become convinced of its truth.

It's not that p.k.'s are more spiritually minded, academically superior, or necessarily better networked (though that should not be discounted). The primary reason they often do better in local church ministry is they have grown up with an almost instinctive grasp of traditional church life in America.

Begin to note how many effective pastors in existing churches (not church plants) are either p.k.'s, grandchildren of pastors, or have married a pastor's daughter. You'll be astounded at the percentages. Pulpit committees of churches needing turnaround would do well to take a hard look at this variable.

A man I respect highly warned against treating the church as an organization instead of an organism. A reading of the New Testament, however, reveals it is both. As an organism, Christ is the head and we are the body. The church is Christ's bride. The members are members of His body. As an organization there must be officers (no organism has officers), as well as rules and protocols.

Seminaries, consciously or otherwise, train pastoral candidates to a greater degree for their participation in the church as an organism than as chosen head over an organization.

Does it offend you to suggest that, next to godliness, political savvy may be the most important ingredient for leading successful turnaround? This will consume our attention in chapters 7-9.

7) *Are you a strategic thinker?*

Are you a chess player? If not, learn (seriously)! Chess, the game of kings, is a metaphor for life and ministry. If you play it enough its lessons will transfer to your modes of thinking.

Some of the strategic principles it teaches include:

- Conflict need not be raucous or physical. Chess is a very civil competition. Two players sit calmly on the outside, while attempting to win an advantage over the other. Such is church life in a turnaround environment.

- Losing your temper is taboo. You forfeit the game if you sweep the pieces off the board.

- The goal is to protect the king at all costs. The king of course represents our Lord Jesus Christ. His interests are really all that matters.

- The pieces on the board have different capabilities. Their value is assigned based upon their perceived potential to defend the king.

- The game is both defensive and offensive. While we move our pieces ahead we must not forget the opposition is moving against us.

- Occasionally pieces should be sacrificed for the ultimate good. Other times pieces are traded.

   Note: I prefer to think of the chess pieces as issues, not people. Not every issue is worth dying for.

- It is possible to regain a lost piece, but it is not probable or to be assumed. Once a piece is lost, let it go. Stay focused.

- You cannot play the game without losing some pieces.

- Every piece moved on the board changes the game permanently and radically.

◆ To win you must always be thinking several steps ahead.

Too often, would-be turnaround leaders forget, or worse, are not even conscious of these principles. Chess is an emotionally demanding game in part because it requires such thought, constant re-evaluation, and self-restraint.

This is what we mean by strategic thinking.

Summary

Review the seven questions in this chapter. Be honest. Your answers will tell you whether you are equipped and ready to tackle the task of turn-around. No one is perfect. All leaders have weaknesses. Are you prepared to repair the chinks in your armor before moving on? Better you recognize them now than your enemies point them out later.

CHAPTER 4

The Ninety-Five Percent Theory

S imply stated the 95 percent theory is that 95 percent of all serious problems in the church stem from a power struggle. This theory is not intended to negate biblical admonitions for reconciliation. In fact, most church leaders are adept at and ready to resolve conflict that arises over petty matters. They deal with personality and trivial issues daily with relatively good success.

Power struggles are a different matter. They are, in fact, by definition fundamentally irresolvable. The question in a power struggle is, who will lead and who will leave? American culture has contributed to the unwillingness of many church leaders to deal with power struggles. Our government functions with a two-party system. There is always one party in power, and a rival party seeking to strip them of this power and place themselves in leadership.

American politics has taught our people checks and balances are necessary. We are frequently reminded that power corrupts and absolute power corrupts absolutely. Due to the fallen nature of man, the two-party system has been implemented to keep leaders honest and prevent abuse of authority. Therefore, one party rules for a time while the other circles over them like a hawk awaiting its prey. Any sign of faltering and they swoop down for the kill. The church has felt the impact of this.

The church, however, was never intended to be a two-party system. The New Testament sets forth the standards for leadership and instructs the congregation to submit to those over them. The pastor, working alongside the governing board, is given the responsibility of establishing direction for the body. As long as the direction is within biblical perimeters, the body is to submit to its duly selected leaders.

Before looking more closely at power struggles within the church, let's ask the broader question: Why do churches fall into decline?

There are five common scenarios which contribute to plateau and decline.

1. External factors beyond the church's control.

    Demographic changes take place due to an economic downturn. Whole segments of the business community shut down causing people to leave the area. Perhaps high crime and decay in the area surrounding the church make people leery of attending the church. A fire or natural disaster may damage the neighborhood.

    If a pastor and board cannot figure out a way to address these unexpected variables, their leadership will be called into question. Walt Wilson, a corporate executive in the Silicon Valley, told me that when a company shows eight quarters of declining profits, it is in trouble. At that time the CEO usually begins to pinpoint external factors beyond his control. From then on, creative suggestions must come from without the company. Pastors, unlike business leaders, are usually unwilling to acknowledge that when their church shows eight quarters or more of decline, their people also begin questioning leadership. The membership recognizes the leaders do not have answers. Someone must step forward to rescue the church. In the absence of competent leadership, self-appointed leaders step forward.

2. A coalition of "unfortuitous circumstances."

    Nonreligious people simply call it bad luck. Those of us with a high view of God's sovereignty prefer to see it as the providence of God permitting coalescing unfortunate events for purposes known only to Himself.

    One example might be when a number of staff members resign in a short period of time for reasons totally unrelated to one another. One is overtaken in moral failure, another moves to a place of ministry more in keeping with his gifts, still another is taken seriously ill. While none of these resignations is the fault of the leadership nor connected, it is naive to think some within the congregation will not begin to question what is taking place.

Another example of "unfortuitous circumstances" would be when a major employer in the community closes its plant, two board members who are major contributors are forced to relocate out of town, and the long-time secretary resigns to spend more time with her family. Around this time the popular volunteer youth leader graduates from college and resigns, causing several high schoolers to go to a youth group at another church nearby. There is no cause and effect relationship in these changes, but the church family nonetheless feels ill at ease about what is happening. The bottom line is a slow decrease in attendance and giving. These members who have been unhappy for some time seize this moment to raise questions about the capability of the pastor. They point to the trend of lower attendance to support their cause.

3. A power struggle which results in the losers leaving.

Two dynamics drive the vast majority of power struggles. The first has best been described by Lyle Schaller as the Pioneer-Homesteader feud. The pioneers are the first to enter unsettled lands. Those who come later to farm the land are called homesteaders. Pioneers and homesteaders always find it difficult to get along with one another. The pioneers feel they have the "first rights" to the land and resent the intrusion of the homesteaders. This occurs in the church too.

Pioneers have a long tenure and close relationships which permit them to control the church. To be fair, they have sacrificed to see the church built and have invested countless hours in caring for the property and the people. They also have a long shared history which binds them together closely.

The homesteaders, on the other hand, have comparatively little appreciation for the history of the church and are most concerned with the here and now. They also bring innovative perspectives and often a desire to implement those ideas that worked well in their previous churches.

The result is a range war. Who will control the land? A new pastor is more likely to identify with the homesteaders than the pioneers. He is usually anxious to move these newer people on to the governing board and is likely to view the pioneers who hold the power as his adversaries.

A second common cause of a power struggle is tension between the senior pastor and another staff member. Sometimes two or more staff members will conspire to remove or undermine the leadership of the senior pastor. The reasons for this insubordination are myriad, but there are several predictable scenarios. First an associate who was there prior to the arrival of the senior pastor and wished to be the preaching pastor, may resent being overlooked. Second, frustrated staff may resent being told what to do. When this happens the struggle takes the form of a labor-management dispute. The power struggle may be initiated by the staff with the intent of removing their boss. What they fail to comprehend is that if he goes, they will still find themselves under the authority of another senior pastor. Finally, a long-time staff member — whether secretary, custodian, worship leader, associate, etc. — may take advantage of his deep relationships and knowledge of how things get done. Usually conflict begins when the senior pastor meddles with the staff members' perks and "assumed rights," though they may not be formally agreed to.

Whatever the cause for the struggle, the "losers" leave. In the above cases the issue of who is in charge is usually not resolved amicably. The staff members leave only because they cannot wrest the authority from the grasp of the pastor and board.

The decline of the church in these cases, however, is normally not seen immediately. The problem begins if the losers of the power struggle don't leave quietly. It is not unusual for the departed person or group to continue to make phone calls, hold home meetings, host social events with a strategic guest list, write letters and stir the pot of discontent among those who have remained. Over time, another member leaves. They adversely affect yet another, and still another. It is the chain reaction which creates the decline. Despite their protests to the contrary, this is precisely what the losers of the power struggle desire.

The tragic but fascinating thing is that often what one departed church member is unhappy about is not the same issue which prompts the next to leave. Sometimes those who end up leaving were formally bitter rivals. But the glue that holds together those leaving is the glue of the common enemy; that is, the church leadership.

Before long, even those who had been positive during the initial conflict are impacted by this cancer of criticism and unhappiness. In such cases the question which eventually surfaces is, "Why are all these good people leaving?"

The smaller the city and the more family connectedness there is in the church the more difficult it is to stop this exiting spiral. Before long most everyone in the conflict has forgotten what the original issues were. All they know is that many people are leaving, and they assume leadership must be doing something wrong.

The emotional drain of going through such a time as this can lead to number four.

4. A power struggle in which the pastor leaves.

Once again the specific causative factors are numerous, but several general scenarios are common.

The pastor often is frustrated into resignation. When I candidated in our second church, I noticed one member had several daughters who were married and remained in the church with their families. I casually commented on that fact. He responded, "Yes, we don't always get our way here, but we can usually stop anything from happening if we don't like it." At least I had fair warning, which is more than many pastors receive.

A pastor knows he is expected to lead the church in effective outreach. He realizes his ability to attract new people to the church will be a primary basis for evaluation of his clerical success or failure. When his attempts to bring new people into the church are continually stymied by the hostile critical environment, it is often more than he can cope with. He resigns.

Recently our denomination asked me to serve as its national spokesman for our 1200 churches. Part of the charge was to "fan the flame" and be a "fire lighter" amongst our pastors for evangelism and discipleship. As part of my responsibilities I taught a seminar subtitled: "When you begin to fan the flame, the bucket brigades will not be far behind." The response of pastors to this seminar was overwhelming. It seems every church has someone who believes it is his or her responsibility to douse the red hot coals of the pastor's enthusiasm, sometimes to the point of resignation.

Four of the bucket brigades we talk about are:

(1) The Analyzer Brigade. These people never say an outright "no" to any proposal, they simply demand it go back to committee for evaluation and fine tuning. They love process more than the product. This

paralysis of analysis drains the leader's time and energy and usually slows progress.

(2) The Traditional Brigade. These are the historians in the church. Whenever a creative program is introduced, they can tell when such a concept was tried and invariably why it did not work. On the other hand, they insist upon hanging on to some programs and methods because they worked exceptionally well in 1950. This group is famous for the seven deadly words of the church, "We've never done it that way before."

I sat in one trustee meeting in which we were discussing the need to tear down a 1890's vintage building. One second generation member objected: "That building was good enough for me and my brother. I don't understand why kids cannot use it today." He evidently missed the point. It was worn out and outdated precisely because it had served so many generations.

(3) The Pietist Brigade. "Just pray and God will do it," they exhort. Interpretation: They see no need for planning, goal setting or brain-storming about how to better reach the community.

"Just preach the Word," translates into, "You do the preaching, Pastor, and we will take care of the administrative decisions."

Years ago I pastored a church which was over 130 years old. I jokingly tell friends we still had some charter members. One of these long entrenched members was on the board. Rick also happened to be the church patriarch. Whenever any issue was brought to the board for a decision, anyone was free to share his thoughts, but prior to the vote all eyes turned to Rick. If his head shook up and down, the vote would be a slam-dunk "yes." If it went side to side, the motion would be defeated.

I recommended to the board we do a pictorial directory. It seemed like a good idea for a number of reasons. The board discussed some logistical details for about 15 minutes during which Rick remained absolutely quiet. Finally it was time to vote. All eyes turned to him. He shook his head to indicate disagreement. I had to know why. So I asked, "Rick, what possible reason could you have not to want to do a pictorial directory?"

He thought for a long moment, then said in his most pontifical voice, "I just can't see the early church doing this."

I refrained from pointing out that a directory painted on parchment would have been immensely challenging to reproduce. This type of piety is extremely difficult to combat. All opinions and preferences of the pious ones are couched in spiritual sounding jargon, even if it's absolute balderdash.

(4) The Whining Brigade. These people keep the pastor so busy he has no time to provide leadership which would bring about positive change.

The expectations in one of my earlier churches required me to visit our shut-ins and make hospital calls. One woman demanded I come by to see her once a week. She was seldom in church but often in the hospital. She could enumerate, and often did, her 20-plus surgeries. The doctors had taken just about everything they could out of her. I sat hours on end listening to her "organ recital" because I thought she would soon be deceased. I recently went back to that city. Fourteen years had passed. Her husband, a good, hard-working man, is now with the Lord but she is still alive.

Many individuals, such as the one just described, will call their friends on the phone to see if the pastor has been by to see them. They are keeping score of pastoral visits. Such expectations of personal attention wear a leader down.

While some of these expectations amount to little more than petty annoyance, the cumulative weight can drive even a strong leader to the point of resignation. These demanding members collectively prohibit the leader from channeling his energies to bring about changes which would allow the body to bear fruit, extinguishing the flame of vision.

Power struggles and progress

I have a sign hung in my office which I see daily. It reads: "People are not against you, they are for themselves."

Because the nature of the attack is not vicious does not mean it is any less a hindrance to the work of God. It is in fact a subtle form of a power struggle. And power struggles inhibit progress. Bucket brigades delight in extinguishing the flame of progress and change.

On occasions when members of the bucket brigades marshal a frontal assault against positive change, it may be appropriate for the pastor to speak directly to them about it, especially if the brigade members are sitting on the board or are in other prominent positions where their obstructionism can hinder forward progress. An example of such a conversation follows:

Pastor Jorgenson talks with his board

Mark Jorgenson graduated with honors from his denomination's premier seminary. He was highly recruited by several churches searching for a forward-thinking pastor. He and his wife Jamie chose Willcreek Congregational Church due in large part to the vision outlined by the pulpit committee. After 14 years of steady decline they told him they knew change was necessary and felt a younger man would be what they church needed to reach its farming community. With their two-year-old daughter the Jorgensons moved with high expectations. They assumed the church understood that change was needed and that it would be open to new ideas. Wrong.

The first year was a honeymoon. The church, which had been averaging close to 125, climbed to an average attendance of 156 within three months. Young couples drove into town from the neighboring city 10 miles away. Offerings were ahead of budget.

Many of the young couples who drove to Willcreek Church were happy with Pastor Mark's preaching but wanted a more contemporary style of worship.

At his fourth board meeting, Pastor Mark suggested it might be encouraging to the new attenders at Willcreek if drums and a bass guitar were added to assist in the morning worship. In fact, several new members were anxious to help. He was not prepared for the response. The board told him the instruments would be alright once in awhile, but that using just the organ and piano on most Sundays would make the congregation more comfortable.

Pastor Mark let it pass. In the ensuing months the board also opposed his proposal to add two more adult Sunday school classes, fearing it might cause some members of long-standing classes to leave them. They also did not respond positively to his idea of a Friday night outreach event in the gym for the community following football games since it might attract the wrong type of kids. As the months wore on, the church continued to grow. When morning attendance reached 210 Mark became concerned that many of the young couples would begin to question their decision to join if their church did not become more open to innovative outreach ideas. After much prayer he decided it was time to have a pastor-board talk.

He prepared the board by asking them to pray every day for the next month. He told them he loved them and the church and would respect their decisions but his heart was troubled. At the next meeting he needed to share his feelings and concerns with them. That Thursday night there was definitely an air of anticipation. After prayer and approval of the agenda he said:

"We all know how the church-pastor relationship works in our culture today. The pastor accepts a call to lead the congregation and moves his family thousands of miles. He asks his children and wife to give up all their friendships, leave their home and begin a new life."

"The expectation of the congregation is that this new pastor's arrival will mark a fresh beginning for the church. They are counting on him to bring them vision and hope."

"I have now brought to this board several viable recommendations for enhanced ministry to our neighborhood. You have determined none of my recommendations are right for the church. Perhaps you have better suggestions. If so, I would invite you to lay them out on the table so we can consider them. Good ideas do not need to be my ideas. But the main thing—fulfilling our purpose statement—is not negotiable."

"Here is what we all know. If after a few years I am unable to move this church forward in a positive manner, the unspoken expectation is that I will be expected to move on. That means I must once again face the unpleasant task of moving my family to another location and asking them to start their lives over again."

"Now I do not mind risking failure. If the suggestions and recommendations I bring to you all fail to produce fruitful results, then perhaps I should not be your leader. But I would at least like to fail doing what I think is best, not because you have prohibited our church from moving ahead."

"If you insist upon blocking all my recommendations for constructive change, there is one other alternative. Possibly you have some creative ideas. Bring them to the board. If they don't go well . . . then you can sell your home and move to another town and ask your family if they would like to begin a new life."

"What do you think we should do?"

Pastor Mark's experience is shared to highlight in graphic terms the frustration many pastors feel. Turnaround leaders are not afraid to talk about the obvious. This is better than allowing the flame of vision and creativity to be doused repeatedly without addressing unreasonable obstructionism.

When pastors resign under unpleasant circumstances, the problems remain and the church begins a prolonged process of decay and decline. This serves no helpful purpose for church or pastor.

5. A power struggle which is cloaked with denial.

Denial is not a river in Egypt. The line in many churches has been drawn. No one is willing to blink. The battle rages furiously beneath the surface. Votes are predictably split, and no one wishes to budge. Every new member is systematically recruited by the opposing sides. New members are either sucked into the fray or choose to move to another church free from acrimony.

Of course, such a battlefield does not produce a climate for growth. Year after year services are held, positions filled, bulletins printed, musical events hosted and missionary presentations given. But all is done in an atmosphere of distrust. It's a pitiful facade. This is playing church at its worst.

Churches stuck in such a state of denial frequently find the senior pastor pitted against a church bully. For some inexplicable reason, the congregation does not want to confront this person (male or female), though this entrenched lay person obstinately opposes the church's making any radical change, even if it means the change would give the church a chance to thrive again.

William M. Easum has written an excellent article titled *On Not Being Nice For the Sake of the Gospel* (Net Results, April 1997). This insightful church consultant writes:

"Courageous pastors often ask, 'What do I do with one or two persons who intimidate the church so much that it is not willing to try something new?' My response is always, 'Either convert them, neutralize them, kick them out, or kill them. The body cannot live with cancer.'"

Easum explains the frustration the church feels not only with the bully, but with leadership that is unwilling to confront the situation.

> Almost every struggling church has at least one dysfunctional bully who goes out of the way to be a big fish in a small pond. Often, that is the primary reason the church is struggling. This person gets a sense of self-worth by keeping the church so intimidated, either by actions or money, that very little can happen without the person's approval. The sad thing is that most of the leaders know this person presents a stumbling block to the church's future, but they will not do anything about it. The church leaders ignore the bully thinking that is the Christian thing to do. In so doing they assist in the congregation's stunted growth or decline.

Easum is profoundly, though tragically, correct. In chapter 5 we will address the worst case offenders and provide suggestions for identifying and dealing with them.

Why power struggles are irresolvable

At the beginning of the chapter, I stated power struggles are fundamentally irresolvable. I don't expect everyone to agree with this. In fact many who argue most adamantly may in truth be the very ones who desire to use power struggles to keep their churches from becoming healthy, or are leaders who know if the power struggle were removed, they would lose their favorite excuse for ineffectiveness.

Yes, some pastors (hopefully unconsciously) contribute to this. As long as pastors allow conflict to keep them from succeeding, they deflect blame from themselves for failure. Chapters seven through nine discuss 12 steps turnaround pastors take to stop perpetual power struggles.

The underlying issue in power struggles is who will determine the direction of the church. Will it be the pastor working alongside of the duly elected lay leadership or a self-appointed minority faction?

An illustration will be helpful. Picture the church as a wagon. A team of large horses has been harnessed to the wagon with instructions from the farmer to pull it in an easterly direction. Does it make sense to harness a second set of horses to the other end and allow them to pull it to the west? No, of course not. Not only will this hinder the first team from achieving the assignment of the owner/farmer, but it will potentially fracture the wagon. Certainly such a ridiculous action makes movement to the east much more difficult.

This, however, is precisely what many pastors allow to happen to their churches. The congregation has called them to lead them to fulfill the purpose of the church, and so pastors simply cannot allow oppositional thinking to be harnessed to the leadership team of the church. When they do, the result is perpetual and predictable split votes. The "issues" are never the issue. The underlying question is, who will lead.

The illustration of the wagon makes for another salient point. Going east is not inherently superior to moving west. The point is: No wagon can move simultaneously in both directions.

Effective turnaround pastors understand this. They do not attempt to make every directional decision a debate between good and evil. All input should be welcomed. But persons who habitually and predictably oppose the direction of the team may need to be cut loose. This is ultimately for their good as well as for the health of the church. It is the loving thing to do.

One factor to look for is the pattern of predictability. Does an individual have a history of obstructionism? Does everyone within the leadership structure know this individual must be appeased or a price be paid? Does this person attempt to intimidate others or exude the attitude "It's my way or else?"

Effective turnaround pastors do not always insist on having their way. They attempt to reach decisions by consensus. They subscribe to the principle: "Bad goals are your goals. Good goals are our goals." They are team players. These pastors appreciate the input and participation of lay-leadership. They work hard to see all involved have adequate opportunity to participate in the development of plans. But having said this, they refuse to allow one difficult person to stand in the way of the main thing.

The wagon must move. Turnaround leaders are obsessed with the shortness of time available to achieve great things for God. They believe their church is a vital part of God's plan to win the lost and will not allow a minority group to hinder what He wants to do among them.

Many church members claim to believe in congregational government but show by their practice they do not. Why are churches so inclined to allow the minority to establish the order of the day? Why do they give cantankerous members more than one vote? When a church acquiesces to the minority, that is what it does.

One means of breaking the back of an ongoing power struggle is to move ahead with the majority. Most status-quo churches are overrun by members with a subconscious desire for continuity and tradition. By moving ahead with the majority decision — despite opposition — the back of tradition-driven thinking is finally broken.

When uncooperative members see their fussing and fuming has not accomplished what they intended, they often see the handwriting on the wall and move on, or at least get out of the way, permitting the church to get on with the business of reaching a lost world for Christ.

Pastor William's difficult conversation

The Stiffer family was well connected. By intermarriage they could name at least 52 attenders within the church with blood ties. Young Gary was brash. He had been raised around the table with conversations which left him convinced it was his family's duty to protect the church from the encroaching liberalism of contemporary culture. The new pastor represented all that his family feared: new music, a more structured congregational meeting which allowed for less free-flowing discussion, an increasing number of new members who did not as yet understand how things were supposed to be done, and a new aerobics class for outreach where the women were permitted to wear gym clothes.

Gary knew something must be done. He stormed into Pastor Williams' office to confront him with the changes that had been taking place at First Church without a congregational vote.

He admitted that no violations of the church constitution had taken place but claimed Pastor Williams had definitely taken unprecedented steps. Gary informed Pastor Williams that his family would not sit quietly and allow these decisions to go unchallenged.

Pastor Williams listened patiently. When Gary was finished he responded, "You may be right and I'm wrong in these issues, but some time ago this congregation called me to be its pastor. As such, I must assume leadership in these decisions. If I don't do so the congregation will have a right to request my resignation because I did not fulfill my calling.

"Now it's possible that they no longer wish me to serve as their leader. I do not believe that to be the case. But you have indicated some doubt about my right to lead. In fact, perhaps they would like you to be the pastor. The only way we can find that out is for you to call a meeting of the body. The process for that is found in our by-laws."

"I have attempted to model submission for this congregation. I want you to know that if indeed the church votes for me to step down, I will be the easiest person they ever got rid of. But in the meantime I must lead, because that is what they have asked me to do. Where we go from here is your call."

Such a response to those who oppose the pastor in the midst of power struggles will emphasize the gravity of what is being played out. This is a serious matter. The future of the church hangs in the balance. Who will lead? Who will leave? They know by such a response that the pastor is very serious. I like to refer to this approach as the *authority of submission*.

Reflections on Pastor Williams' response

One word of caution: A pastor should not resort to the above speech every time someone questions his decisions or judgment call. Many of those who criticize us are our friends. Pastors are not infallible. They should welcome reasoned dissent. There may be better ways to do things. Turnaround pastors are teachable and humble. They don't always demand their own way. They are open to constructive criticism. We are speaking in this chapter of predictable and on-going directional conflict, which indicates a pattern of oppositional thinking. This is the essence of a power struggle.

Summary

Power struggles are by definition irresolvable because ultimately a body can move in only one direction at a time if it is to move together. God's call upon the pastor and board has been confirmed by the will of the congregation. This leadership team has a sacred obligation to the church family to resist minority factions who seek to undermine and derail the direction they are heading.

CHAPTER 5

They Cannot Leave

"They're baaaack!"

"Who? Where? What?" I asked. "Who's back?"

"The Smiths. During the interim, before you came, Pastor, when the church split, they lost the vote and stormed out of the business meeting declaring they would be back some day to pick up the pieces after we shut the doors."

Bud Smith was a pleasant enough gentleman. His biggest fault was his unwillingness to confront Phyllis, his wife with her vicious tongue. She had been a part-time secretary at the church and had used her position to undermine the deacon board, making numerous phone calls which led to the split.

During the year since my arrival at this small church, things had gone well. Attendance had increased 40 percent and it didn't appear the doors would close, but—they were back! One could have cut the tension in the air that Sunday with a knife.

Following evening service on Sunday I asked Ruth, one of our sweet and godly elderly women, what Phyllis Smith's problem was. Her answer was short and pointed: "I think she's demon possessed!" The terseness of the response was so out of character for this self-controlled woman I'm sure the shock registered on my face.

"She's what?"

"You heard me," Ruth replied, "I think she's demon possessed. How else can you explain the damage she has done to our church?"

At age 29, I confess I discounted Ruth's assessment as hyperbole from a wounded heart. After 17 years of pastoring in three locations, I'm more inclined to believe she may have expressed great insight.

In each church I have encountered one or more individuals who fit a predictable profile. Interaction with pastoral colleagues affirms these people are in their churches also.

Harry was a perpetual source of irritation and turmoil for three of my predecessors. My immediate predecessor and friend, now in Oregon, called me to chat shortly after I arrived in our new church. I asked him about Harry. He laughed and filled me in on some of the history. Then he said, "You know, I think Harry's brother is in our church here in Oregon." We both laughed. Changing churches does not allow us to avoid *those who cannot leave*. Let's begin with a profile. I suspect you have met one or more along the path of your ministry.

Have you met these people?

- ◆ **They have been a member of a particular local church for 20 years or more**.

- ◆ **They have not been pleased with or supportive of any of their pastors**. If you visit with previous pastors, this is confirmed. The conflict the current pastor has with them is similar (even identical) with what his predecessors experienced.

- ◆ **They have little respect for elected layleaders**. If the board supports the senior pastor *those who cannot leave* refer to them as "yes men."

- ◆ **Growth does not excite them**. *Those who cannot leave* attack any serious emphasis upon outreach as preoccupation with numbers. They are fond of reminding us that God has called us to be faithful, not successful. To them success is synonymous with small.

- ◆ **They have never seen a building program they liked**.

- ◆ **They detest new music**. They may express their distaste by only standing to sing if the song selection meets their approval.

Occasionally they ceremoniously walk from the auditorium in the middle of worship.

- **They affect a pained look**. Possibly they complain of backaches or headaches. Their face reflects extreme discomfort.

- **They express a love for *foreign* missions**. Some withhold their financial support from the general fund and claim they will send their money "where it will be used properly." They delight to inform missionaries as to the perceived woes of the church back home. (Note: They seemingly are unconcerned with reaching their own neighborhood.)

- **Their body language is defiant**. While the pastor preaches, they either feign sleep (which is amusing because they manage to catch any faux pas), sit with arms folded, or stare at their feet.

- **They expect to be consulted on every church decision whether in leadership or not**.

- **They are often overweight**. This may be a visual demonstration that *those who cannot leave* lack self-control.

- **When on a concerted oppositional campaign, they will spend entire Sunday mornings floating in the foyer, patio, or parking lot spreading discontent without so much as even attending the worship service**.

- **They cannot comprehend why they are not considered for leadership in the church**.

- **Whenever there is a problem arising in the church, they are not far away**.

- Though perpetually unhappy . . . *they cannot leave*!

If 10 or more of the above characteristics match someone in your church, they fit the *cannot leave* profile.

Discerning the cause

Most church members disagree over some issue, major or minor. Occasionally our convictions prompt us to voice, and even vote, our displeasure. We may even be led by the Spirit of God to remove ourselves from membership and relocate to another fellowship in which we can minister more comfortably. Such behavior is not evil. If pastors are called by God to move to a new ministry, then it is logical to believe church members are as well. Such prayerful and reasoned movement, however, is precisely what makes the pattern of *those who cannot leave* more noteworthy.

Most people reason, "If I am truly unhappy and going to church makes me miserable and I believe my church is heading in the wrong direction, I will express my convictions in a forceful and appropriate manner. If I cannot be part of the solution, I will not be part of the problem." They consequently seek another place of fellowship where they escape weekly emotional and spiritual trauma so as to once again experience the joy of their salvation. This is normal. Such a decision is made by thousands of believers.

Contrasted with this normal behavior is that of *those who cannot leave*. They are miserable! The unhappiness shows on their faces. They seemingly torture themselves by going to a place which they despise. Furthermore, they want everyone to know how displeased they are and join them in being miserable. They sit weekly and listen to the counsel of a man they don't respect. They contribute token financial support to an organization which they believe is headed in a wrong direction. Does this make sense? Why do they put themselves through such agony?

Common explanations

If asked, *those who cannot leave* will tell you it is because *they are committed*. Often they say, "This is my church. I have seen pastors come and go, but I'm still here." The obvious question is: What are they committed to?

I once lived near a major intersection which passed under a railroad trestle. Thousands of pigeons made this trestle their home. It sheltered them from blazing sun in the summer and from the cold Midwestern winters. In time, the structure was torn down. But those birds remained at the intersection with only exposed wires to cling to. They were committed to their home. The reason for selecting the location was removed — but they were committed. Each day on my way home from work, I observed dead pigeons lying in the intersection. I assume a few smart birds found a new location which met their needs.

Another possible reason for the disgruntled's tenacity is they are just *pervasively unhappy people*. Their discontent, as acted out at church, is also displayed in every sphere of their lives. They are dissatisfied at home, work, school, and in the community. Perhaps. But, in the other arenas of life, they are trapped. The choice of churches, however, is free. It is a simple and uncomplicated matter to find another good church.

A third common explanation is that the church is *the last place they can exercise control.* They have unfulfilling careers and home life. The church offers a forum where they can wield influence and be a somebody. This might be plausible except it is difficult to explain their persistence after they have disenfranchised themselves from the membership. Even when they lose influence, the negative crusade continues.

None of the above explanations satisfactorily account for the obstinate resolve of *those who cannot leave.*

A frightening possibility

As our heavenly Father calls his servants to pastor a particular *church*, Satan calls his followers to a mission of disruption and division in a local assembly. *They cannot leave because your church is their assignment.* They are commissioned with a calling to prevent effective ministry from happening. To leave is failure. Such desertion of duty could mean discipline at the hands of their master. Only this reality would appear to account for their irrational determination to prevent progress. Thousands of pastors and dedicated board members who have faced these people will agree.

The admission of such a possibility may appear harsh and judgmental. But before dismissing this thesis, consider the biblical evidence.

- ◆ **Satan is the great counterfeiter** (2 Corinthians 11:13-15). This passage specifically cautions the local church at Corinth to be on the watch for "false apostles, deceitful workers who are *disguising* themselves . . ." It is not to surprise us if ". . . his (Satan's) servants *disguise* themselves as servants of righteousness." Satan can certainly do more damage from within the church than from without. The key to successful infiltration is a clever disguise. The disguise in question here is the appearance of a concerned churchman.

- ◆ **Discord and strife are not of God** (James 3:13-18). It could not be more plain. Factions and strife in the family of God are ". . . not from above, but are earthly, natural, demonic . . . wisdom from above is first pure, then *peaceable, gentle, reasonable. . .*" Satan knows the most effective way to prevent a church from attracting the lost is to create friction and discontent, and to destroy harmony. He accomplishes this by assigning *those who cannot leave* to attend every service, prayer meeting, business meeting and social function.

- **Our battle is spiritual** (Ephesians 6:12). Why should anyone be surprised the enemy would place demonized ambassadors in each local church? He is simply mirroring the pattern of Christ who strategically places gifted individuals within each church for the building up of the saints. Satan's "gifted men" work to tear down the body.

- **Pastors and elders are admonished to be diligent in opposing these people** (Acts 20:28-30). Twice in Paul's parting words to the leaders at Ephesus, he makes it clear the appointees of Satan will attempt to damage the family of God from within ("come in among you; among your own selves").

- **Jesus predicted impostors will always be a part of our local churches** (Matthew 13:24-30). In the parable of the wheat and the tares, Jesus warned that poisonous pretenders will grow among the healthy stalks of wheat. The tares look identical to the wheat. The two can only be distinguished by examining the fruit they bear.

What should we do?

- **Accept the reality**. Not everyone who pretends to be a part of God's family is in fact on God's side. A life-style of unrepentant disruption and divisiveness is the manifest fruit of the enemy. Perhaps the single greatest warning sign that you may be dealing with *one who cannot leave* is his or her hatred for designated authority in the church. Anarchy was the root cause for Satan's expulsion from heaven. Stop being incredulous that Satan works to disrupt the body from within. Face reality. The Scriptures teach it. Experience validates it.

- **Teach the relevant Scriptures to lay leadership**. Of course we need to exercise caution. We don't want to launch into a witch hunt. Not everyone with opposing viewpoints is a tool of Satan. Church members have both the right and obligation to offer opinions. As believer-priests each member receives insight into the will of the Lord. Opportunity must be given for reasoned dissent. But most boards are too reluctant to admit and deal with long-standing, predictable patterns of discord.

♦ **Be slow to question another's profession of faith.** The parable in Matthew 13:24-30 concludes with the landowner instructing his servants not to attempt to separate the tares from wheat. The danger of accidentally cutting out the wheat is too great a risk. The servants are rather to "allow both to grow together until the harvest." When Christ returns He will distinguish perfectly. To harm a child of God by false accusation is serious business. The Lord said it would be preferable to hang a large stone around our neck and throw ourselves into the sea than be guilty of such mishap. It's preferable to deal with a divisive member as an errant brother or sister rather than question his/her salvation. Once you attack a member's profession of faith, you have embarked upon a course which may be deleterious to the health of the body.

♦ **Be prepared to deal with the heinous sin of divisiveness**. The church appears unwilling to deal with this sin. Yet Scripture has much to say concerning it (Proverbs 6:14, 19; 2 Corinthians 12:20; 1 Timothy 6:4; 2 Timothy 2:23). In fact, it is grounds for dismissal from the fellowship (Titus 3:9-11). Seldom will the offender admit to wrongdoing. Instead, he will argue his right to offer contrasting opinion. I once confronted a man. He had been practicing divisive intimidation behavior in the church for decades. I explained to him his actions were disruptive, carnal, and childish. I told him I was tired of it and the church would not tolerate it any longer. I assured him I was prepared to proceed with whatever steps necessary within the perimeters of biblical and constitutional allowances. He was livid. He began to shake, and I honestly thought he might strike me. He eventually stepped close to me and muttered: "I have been in this church for 60 years . . . and . . . no pastor has ever talked to me like this!" I replied, "Yes, and that is precisely the problem! I am. Now, what are you going to do about it?" He is not disrupting that church any longer. He left. When you boldly confront *those who cannot leave*, you may lose members who are in sympathy with them. But the damage of allowing their behavior to go unchecked will be significantly greater. Negativism unhindered is a cancer in the body. Confront biblically. Follow the guidelines in your by-laws. Be patient. But deal with it.

- **Never promote divisive people to leadership**. You may not be able to prevent their membership, but astute and courageous leadership can usually assure these individuals have no leadership role. It is simply bizarre how many pastors place disruptive people into key roles of influence believing it will change them. It doesn't. Instead they then have a platform of influence and credibility to spread their destructive attitude. The congregation assumes those in positions of leadership have the blessing of the church. Those who assign leaders have a responsibility to the congregation to assure biblical qualifications have been met.

A final word

The local church is the body of Christ. To His church has been handed the mission of invading the domain of darkness. The master counterfeiter has reversed the mission. Satan has commissioned his own to put on sheeps' clothing and infiltrate the ranks of Christendom. To the spiritual shepherds belongs the grave task of dealing with those who come in among us to destroy the flock. May we be true to our calling.

NOTE TO THE PASTOR:

This chapter is taken from a booklet we give to all new members at Grace Church, Glendora. As a church reaches and then surpasses the predictable numeric plateaus mentioned in chapter one, the senior pastor's role must change. Unfortunately, church members often don't accept this fact. This may, in fact, assert pressure and demands upon their pastor which curtail the likelihood of further growth.

Furthermore unrealistic expectations upon a pastor by his people lead to his burnout. He attempts to administrate a growing paid staff, visit the sick, oversee expanded programming, preach, lead the evening and midweek service, follow up on visitors, and be available to all the committees and boards. Eventually, like a car running for hours at red-line, something gives.

As you approach a plateau it makes sense to approach your governing board with this issue of over-demand and openly discuss what their expectations are.

This chapter has been laid out to permit easy copying. If after reading it you feel it might be helpful to share it with your board please feel free to photocopy whatever number you need. It should make a wonderful discussion starter for you and your leaders.

Best wishes,

Gene

CHAPTER 6

What Can You Expect From Your Pastor?

Perspective is Everything

It's strange, but my eyes always see things from my point of view. I view the world through my perspective. In fact, one quickly realizes *perspective* is pretty much everything in life.

I read recently that the Audubon Society has discovered a group of intellectual swallows. These birds are doing research on why people return to Capistrano at the same time every year . . . or, perhaps you've heard of the bumper sticker seen on a car in Brighton, England: PAUL REVERE WAS A SNITCH!

Nowhere does one's perspective weigh heavier in local church life than in how members view their pastors. Let's be candid: when you say, "He is a *good* pastor," you really are saying, "He meets my expectations as to what a pastor ought to be and do." The comment, "He is a *bad* pastor," is saying, "He does *not* meet my expectations as to what a pastor ought to be and do."

This whole area is critical to church health. All church growth consultants agree that the pastor-people relationship is a leading (if not *the* preeminent) factor in determining whether a body will be effective. If the constituency of the church believes their pastor is doing what he ought, they will gladly follow him. When people follow their pastor, good things happen. All of us have heard horror stories. The Jim Jones tragedy has become proverbial among modern America. Each of us knows of a dictator who ruined a perfectly healthy church. Nonetheless, the Scripture seems to be quite clear that God wants pastors to lead. When you discover a growing church, you find strong pastoral leadership. You also discover a willing "followership" within the congregation. What causes intelligent, gifted people to follow? The answer is simple: trust. What creates trust? The people perceive that their pastor *is what he ought to be* and *is doing what he ought to be doing*.

A pastor had just read his resignation. He was accepting another call. After the service he greeted people at the door. One of the elderly saints approached him, her eyes swimming with tears. She sobbed, "Oh, Pastor, I'm so sorry you've decided to leave. Things will never be the same again." The pastor was flattered, but equal to the situation. Taking her hands in his, he said, "I'm sure God will send you a new pastor even better than I." She choked back a sob, "That's what they all said, but they keep getting *worse* and *worse*."

The causes of pastor-people problems may be:

◆ The pastor himself. Moral and doctrinal failings are not uncommon.

◆ A contentious spirit on the part of the members. An exiting member bemoaned to her friend, "I don't understand it. I've had five pastors and have experienced problems with every one of them." Some church members do develop an adversarial relationship with every pastor. The issues may be philosophy, vision, or values.

◆ Faulty, unrealistic, or divergent expectations as to what a pastor ought to be.

Let's examine briefly what God's Word says about pastors.

The Scriptures and the pastor

The first two causes require another treatise. Let's now deal with the third. What absolutes are there in God's Word?

1. A pastor should sense a *desire* for the position (1 Timothy 3:1). Pity the congregation where the pastor is continually groaning and living a pity party. The old advice to young men considering the ministry, "If you can do anything else and be happy, do it," is good advice. Around

Grace staff members frequently remind one another, "This sure beats working, doesn't it?" Obviously, this is said in jest. The ministry involves long hours. A 60-hour work week is not unusual.

The word "desire" (oregomai) means "to stretch one's self, reach out after; long for." When God calls a man to pastoral ministry, He implants a burning passion for the work. This desire is supernatural in both its intensity and motive. He feels he can do nothing else. This calling will be displayed in industrious labor and a grateful spirit.

2. He will *meet the qualifications* as set forth in 1 Timothy 3:2-7 and Titus 1:5-9.

3. He will *oversee* the church as a shepherd does his flock (John 21:16; Acts 20:28; 1 Peter 5:2).

To oversee the church involves many things:

- ◆ Acts 20:29-30. Paul exhorts the Ephesian elders (pastors) to *protect* the flock.

- ◆ Titus 1:9. Paul encourages young Titus to *guard* the truth from perversion and error which would take the people into apostasy.

- ◆ 1 Peter 5:2. *Feeding* the flock is enjoined. An obvious reference to expositional teaching and preaching.

- ◆ 1 Peter 5:3. The pastor is to be an *example* to the flock. Sheep are followers by nature. They will go where they are led. They cannot be pushed and shoved.

- ◆ 1 Timothy 3:4-5, 5:17; Hebrews 13:7. The pastor is to *rule* over his flock. While being humble, gentle and fair, he is not to shirk his responsibility to discipline and rebuke.

- ◆ Ephesians 4:11-12. He is to *equip* the people so they will effectively carry on the ministry of the church. Obviously, the responsibility of pastoring is difficult and often thankless. The Scripture is clear that no man would want such a task unless called by God.

The pastor's role and church growth

So far, we've said two things. First, whether or not your pastor is a "good" pastor in your eyes will be determined by what you believe he *ought* to be doing. Second, we've noted what the Scriptures say he ought to do. He is to *protect, guard, feed, set an example, rule,* and *equip.*

The Bible says very little, however, as to *how* he will do each of these things. In fact, the manner in which your pastor will perform these ministries will be largely determined by the *size of your church.* Hopefully the following illustrations and descriptions will assist you in determining what size church you and your family will choose.

Church A (35-100 in morning attendance)

Churches with fewer then 35 in attendance usually do not have full-time pastors. When attendance reaches between 50 and 75, most groups begin to think of hiring someone to shepherd them.

The pastor in such a church is often a soft, gentle, people-person. He, of course, knows everyone by first and last name. He visits every hospital-ized member. He sits with the family when surgery is being done. He knows the ages of your children and may very well remember the names of your pets. He is also most willing to visit your relatives and friends if they are in the hospital.

When church workdays take place, he is the first one there and the last to leave. This pastor frequently cleans the church building and may mow the yard. He often lives next door to the church in a property purchased in case of future expansion. Your pastor plans the bulletins and may, in fact, type them and run them off himself. He is always available and would think nothing of returning home from vacation if someone were seri-ously ill.

He is a friend. Not only will he be in each member's home every year, but often socializes with members—possibly on a weekly basis.

To have anyone else do a funeral or wedding for a church member would be a personal affront to him. Making an appointment with this pastor is all right for "outsiders," but you know he wants you to call or stop by anytime.

To have this type of personal relationship with your pastor, you are willing to make a few sacrifices. You accept the fact it is difficult to attract new people. The dreamed-of expansion just never seems to come. Outreach is difficult because all energy is needed to maintain the church. It is diffi-cult to attract couples with children (especially teenagers). They want a church with a youth program. While you try to persuade them to stay and help build that youth program, they never do.

At times you wish the music program was a little better. The same people sing or play each week—and you've quit trying to get Aunt Mildred to give up the piano. It's okay most of the time, but when you invite your boss or neighbors to church you must secretly admit it is a little embarrassing.

The pastor's time in Church A is divided something like this:

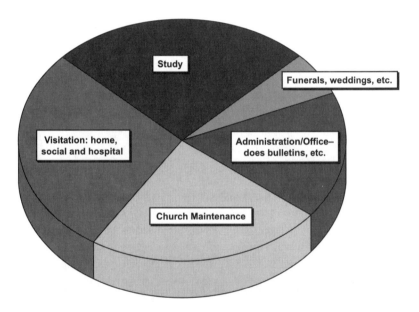

Church A (35–100 in morning attendance)

Church B (100-250)

This pastor is paid a livable wage and does not need outside employment. He *really* is full-time. In fact, occasionally people talk about his needing some paid help. Not everyone is convinced, but the general consensus is that he does. He either has a part-time or full-time secretary.

If the church hires staff, it will likely be a youth pastor. It's unlikely you can pay him enough to live on, and he probably won't stay long.

The Church B pastor still knows your name. He knows your children, but is a bit hazy on your out-of-town relatives. This is a bit disconcerting—you've had to tell him about your grandmother's health problems several times. He visits in your home, but usually not for social reasons. In fact, you've noticed that when he stops by there's either a problem to be smoothed over or he's recruiting you for an office or ministry. It appears he spends more time with key leaders.

The quality of literature has improved with the addition of a secretary. However, it's a bit annoying to call the church and talk to her instead of the pastor. At times you've called and she has informed you he's busy studying. You had to call back later to reach him. While you understand that, you hope it doesn't happen too frequently.

As you approach 250 this pastor becomes "distracted." On a couple of occasions you may have tried to speak with him about your heartaches before church. He seemed preoccupied. You wondered if he cared about you. He seems to be talking about goals and administrative issues.

At this stage (250) you expect your pastor to be competent in the pulpit. Not only do you expect his messages to be accurate, but you judge him on his style.

You discover your pastor would like you to set up an appointment to see him. He is still sometimes available when you drop in—but you can't count on it. More and more emphasis is placed on scheduling things. It is known he is doing a "considerable amount of counseling," a term you didn't hear when things were smaller. He accepts a few spontaneous invitations to go out following church; however, you can't count on him.

The Church B pastor's time is allocated something like this:

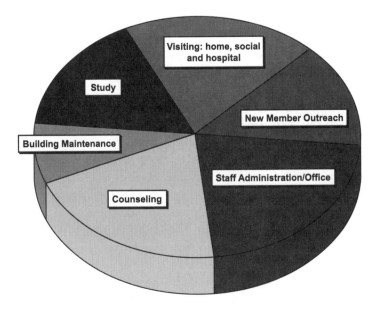

Church B (100–250 in morning attendance)

Note: Major changes from Church A are that he spends less time visiting in homes and more time in counseling (by appointment). He is slowly increasing the time in office administration and decreasing hands-on clerical work and building maintenance.

This is a nice size church. It's big enough to offer some type of program for each age, but still small enough to know almost everyone. Normally, bills are being paid comfortably. It is so nice, 80 percent of churches elect to stay below the next level.

Church C (250-400)

This pastor may have been instrumental in making you feel welcome and wanted in the church when you were new. Possibly, he even visited in your home when you first tried the church. Once you joined, however, you seldom saw him outside of appointments made with him in the office, the pulpit, board/committee meetings or medium/large church social gatherings.

Of course you know he still cares about you, but you accept his busyness. You become aware your pastor is serving on other boards outside the local church. From time to time he is asked to speak elsewhere. While you are pleased others recognize his value, possibly you begin to feel a bit possessive. After all, he is your pastor—or is he? There are occasions when he is unavailable even for funerals and hospital visits. His role is now to train others to shepherd. The expectations of the pastor in Church C are relatively high. He is expected to use good grammar. He should be knowledgeable of current events and be able to interact within varying social and educational strata. Because your friends and relatives may only see him in the pulpit, the least he can do is not embarrass you there.

Staff begin to pick up many of the ministerial responsibilities the pastor did in Church A and B. The pastor not only does not run the office equipment, but you probably hope he'll not touch it. (He'd probably break it!) The pastor is expected to develop the staff and lead it in a spirit of unity and harmony. You beg your pastor not to pick up a hammer. You're paying him too much for him to be doing secretarial or maintenance work.

Increasingly, he becomes a symbolic leader, more of a coach than a star player. Most likely he does not often preach on Sunday nights and his role changes on Wednesdays.

As you near the 400 plateau, he still knows all the members (after 4 to 5 years) but is a bit hazy on the extended church family. He doesn't seem to know the ages of the kids and, frankly, cannot remember your dog's name.

His schedule might look like this. Note how quickly home visits have given way to office and staff oversight. He spends most of his time *equipping others* to do ministry.

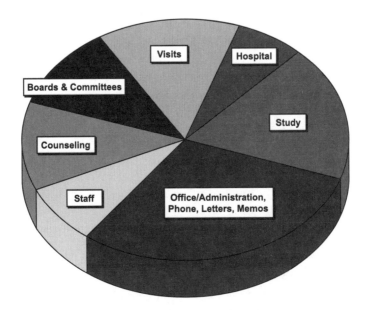

Church C (250–400 in morning attendance)

Church D (400-800)

Less than 5 percent of America's churches proceed to this level of growth. There are a number of reasons for this. Our sole focus here is the role of the pastor.

The pastor in Church D (400+ active attenders) must produce in the pulpit. It has well been said, "His people will forgive him for anything but preaching poorly."

As a church member you no longer expect to socialize with the pastor—certainly not one on one, and if so, not with any regularity. You accepted that when you joined such a church. You do demand he be well educated. He had best know administrative and time management principles. He operates by an appointment calendar. Your pastor will probably no longer make hospital visits unless you're a key church leader, or it's quite a serious injury or illness. Other staff and lay ministers must now do the routine hospital, shut-in, and caring ministries which are so important. The member in Church D understands and accepts this.

It may appear, to those in smaller churches, that you have sacrificed too much to belong to a large church. You, however, know better. Yes, you have minimized a relationship with one brother in the Lord (your pastor), but you believe he still *feeds, protects, models, and equips*; maybe not directly, but through others. You know there are gifted men and women on the church staff who love you. Members of the body are trained to do evangelism, hospital visitation, even counseling.

You're proud to invite your friends to church. The music is good. Programs are offered for all ages and a variety of special needs. The church facilities accommodate recreational activities. Camps, banquets, M.O.P.S., AWANA, Tough Love, support groups for singles, drug-alcohol dependency, and numerous other ministries make *your* church a full-service institution. You consider sharing your pastor a small price for what it offers you and your family.

The Church D pastor's time is allotted like this:

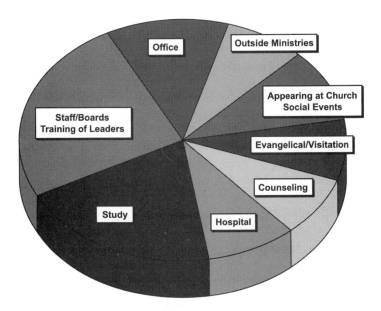

Office

Outside Ministries

Appearing at Church
Social Events

Staff/Boards
Training of Leaders

Evangelical/Visitation

Counseling

Study

Hospital

Church D (400-800 in morning attendance)

<u>Church E</u> (800-1200)

The pastor cannot personally shepherd everyone in the church. In fact, he will not know everyone who attends. His ministry is exemplary and symbolic. He models a healthy marriage. He exemplifies holiness. He models worship. He models caring. He models evangelism; however, in this arena, he cannot grow the church on the basis of who he can personally lead to Christ.

His priorities are:

- be intimate with God

- disciple and be intimate with his own family

- shepherd the board and their families

- shepherd and administrate the pastoral/ministry staff

- preach the Word

At Grace the elder board has gone on record to state they do not expect their senior pastor to do one-on-one member care. *They* will do that part of the ministry. Staff and board members will do the hospital, shut-in, and house calling as needed. The senior pastor's responsibility is to see that they are adequately organized and equipped for such ministry. The elders have also committed themselves to handling baptismal and membership interviews as well as problems which arise. In short, they will function as lay staff.

Lyle Shaller refers to the church as a mini-denomination, an apt description of what is taking place at Grace Church of Glendora each week. Each Sunday morning four congregations meet on the Grace campus: 8:15, Celebration (contemporary worship); 9:30, Adoration (traditional worship); 10:45, Connection (contemporary with an interactive twist); 10:45, Hispanic worship (in Spanish).

At a church of this size, the pastor is recognized as the church's CEO. Paper is king, memos abound, newsletters are the primary means of church-wide communication, computers hum, staff meetings are a necessity, budgets grow exponentially and specialized ministries begin like heating popcorn. Your pastor is not involved in all ministries but is expected to have a handle on each facet of the ministry.

The Church E pastor's time is allotted like this:

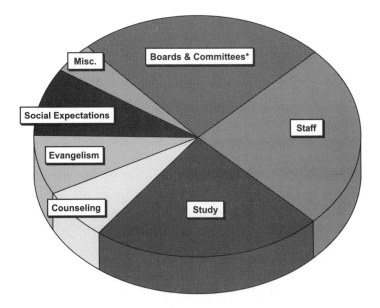

Church E (800-1200 in morning attendance)

*both inside and outside the local church

When a congregation averages over 800 in morning worship attendance, it becomes more difficult to generalize how the pastor uses his time. There are so few of these churches, and each is somewhat unique. Lyle Schaller says that while the number is growing and probably will continue to grow rapidly, these churches represent only 2 percent of the 350,000 Protestant congregations in the United States.

Precisely how the senior pastor expends his time will be determined by several variables:

- His spiritual gift mix

- The length of time the church has been this size

- The number of sermon preparations he does

- The ability of his staff to function independently

- The financial resources the church has available to hire staff

- His involvement in kingdom work outside the church

The church can continue to grow **if** its members are willing to support the Pyramid Principle, and **if** they are willing to accept the fact member care must come from somewhere other than the senior pastor.

Pyramid Principle

Leading a church from one size to the next demands tangible steps of faith. I have found the following illustration immeasurably helpful.

Picture in your mind a large table standing on four legs. A dump truck backs up to the table and proceeds to dump a load of sand on to it. As the sand falls, it eventually takes on the shape of a pyramid. At some given point the table is full. You can dump additional sand on the pyramid, but it will fall off the sides of the table. You might try to hose down the sand so more sand will stick but as it dries the sand falls off because the table is full.

If you picture the local church as a table, the same principle holds true in regards to the number of people it can accommodate. As God sends men and women, boys and girls to visit the local church, they attempt to find a place on the table. But as the pyramid (i.e., the people being retained and ministered to) reaches maximum size, people begin to fall off the edges. The pyramid is full.

Now, rather than patting and hosing the sand and going around picking the sand up, it makes sense to expand your base; that is, to increase the size of the table.

In a local church, the base consists of three things:

- ◆ Facilities

- ◆ Staff (paid and volunteer)

- ◆ Programs and ministries of the church

Faith must precede sight. Always. Expand the base of ministry first. The Lord will send people to a church prepared to give quality care to them. I strongly encourage you to keep your eyes open for Dave Womack's book titled *The Pyramid Principle of Church Growth* (Minneapolis: Bethany Fellowship, Inc., 1977). It is worth searching for.

CHAPTER 7

Characteristics of Turnaround Leaders

So far we've argued that the principles that can guide a church back to health and fruitfulness are transferable. We have encouraged the would-be leader to frankly evaluate himself in seven major areas in chapter three. Chapter four explained the 95 percent rule. Power struggles are at the core of virtually every declining church. Some within the church would rather bury it than forfeit the privilege of having their own way. Chapter 5 dealt with some unusually difficult types found in most dying churches, and chapter 6 encouraged the pastor to act his size.

We now turn our attention to some of the transferable principles and practices normally discovered in turnaround successes. Each may be learned, improved, and eventually inculcated as habits if we are willing.

#1) Turnaround leaders consider leadership an act of service.

The importance of quality leadership is now universally understood. Because of this, there has been an unprecedented proliferation of writing on the topic in the last decade. A list of books on leadership you may wish to read include:

Your Gift of Administration by Ted Engstrom, (Nashville: Nelson Publishers, 1983). Pastors sometimes feel guilty if they are not "doing." Engstrom helps us understand that administration is work. It is also a spiritual gift given for the health and advancement of the church.

Top Ten Mistakes Leaders Make by Hans Finzel, (Wheaton: Victor Books, 1994). Having worked closely with Hans Finzel, I know first hand he practices what he teaches. He has been instrumental in moving CBInternational into the 21st century and bringing necessary and innovative change to an established organization without alienating the constituency he leads. You'd do well to be familiar with this practitioner.

Leading With Integrity by Fred Smith Sr., (Minneapolis: Bethany House Publishers, 1999). He shares a life time of experience. Reading this book is like sitting at the feet of an American Christian leader-patriarch. His love for the Lord coupled with his no nonsense approach to leadership is practical and refreshing.

Learning to Lead by Fred Smith Sr., (Waco: Word Books, 1986). This book is my personal favorite on leadership. It is out of print, but worth finding. His chapter on time management during peak demand periods of life is priceless. If you're too busy, you need this book.

The Second Coming of the Church by George Barna, (Nashville: Word Publishing, 1998). I recommend this book because it helps us understand the growing syncretism within our churches. Pastoral leadership must address this reality or our churches will become irrelevant.

The 21 Irrefutable Laws of Leadership by John Maxwell, (Nashville: Nelson Publishers, 1998). This book is what the title indicates: a compilation from John's illustration files. However, these stories shed light on the tried and true principles of leadership.

Leading Your Church to Growth by C. Peter Wagner, (Ventura: Regal Books, 1984). While I strongly disagree with his premise that pastors receive revelation from God others in the church may not receive, Wagner's thesis that everything will basically rise and fall on the pastor's ability and willingness to lead makes this book worth owning.

Some of the advice and counsel in these books is conflicting. They all agree, however, that leadership is key. It is not something for which we should apologize. Leadership and administration are hard work. They are gifts given by the Holy Spirit for the building up of his body.

Decline seldom happens overnight. It is the result of a dysfunctional system. A series of decisions and choices made over years cause the church to stop winning the lost to Christ. Members experience a less loving community and true worship exists only in memories, as most recall how wonderful it once was. Those laypeople who were sincerely concerned by the failure of the church to be a "main thing" assembly have long since left.

Those who remain when a senior pastor is called are those who either like the way things are, are oblivious, or have just resigned themselves to live with status quo. That's the reality of what a new pastor inherits in a dying church. Without exception ill churches are inner consumed.

If utility bills are being paid, foreign missions commitments kept, the temperature acceptable, and the lawn mowed, they are content.

How can a new pastor expect to immediately build consensus for growth with such a complacent congregation? Their very participation in the group is evidence of lack of passion for significant change and advancing the Kingdom of God.

Just do it

The pastor needs to face reality. The easiest thing to do upon arrival is assume it is all right for him to be biblical. There are a number of things for which he does not need permission. He does not need a vote to see if he can share the gospel. He does not need permission to disciple those who come to faith, preach passionately, invite others to hold a study in their home for marginally involved people in the church, or expect his congregation to resolve conflict in a biblical manner.

He must be loving, friendly and hospitable. He should visit often in homes if the church has fewer than 300. It is still true a home-going pastor means a church-going people. The pastor does not need to ask permission to do these things. Jesus already told him what to do. The Word of God is our authority. It's amazing how many things get voted on that need not be.

What things can you just do in your church without permission? Do them. Leadership first focuses on what can be done, not what cannot be done. That comes later. Lead yourself! Establish credibility via action not words.

It may be best not to print your intentions in the church letter or declare them in a public address. People will see what you're doing. They've heard all the well-baked strategy plans many times before. They'll welcome action grounded in the Word.

Invite others to do it

Eventually the turnaround leader will need to recruit others to become involved in practicing Christianity. The specifics of the program or ministry are relatively unimportant. Whatever it is, however, it should be a main thing ministry: winning, building, equipping, multiplying. Leaders see little reason to call a meeting or ask a committee. Asking the deacons if he can go with friends to the mall to share Christ is like asking permission to breathe!

In the beginning there is no need to go out of your way to upset the status quo. Leave the existing power base and entrenched programs alone. If the church is dying, tweaking the morning worship service by adding a new chorus won't make much difference.

Whenever possible don't take anything away. Simply add the positive. For example: "You have some wonderful Sunday school classes in place. Let's keep them going. But I'm going to meet with a handful of new believers in my office at the 9:30 hour."

Or "The choir is doing terrific (all three members), but we have two new couples who love to sing and will be going down to the retirement center on Sunday afternoon to minister. Sometime we may ask them sing on Sunday so we can all enjoy their talents."

Leadership by addition is almost always preferable to replacement. It requires no permission. The old established ministries must be maintained for a time to silence opposition. In a seriously declining church, however, an energetic pastor should be able to maintain those in his sleep. Keep the existing plates spinning to demonstrate there is no loss, only additions and gain.

Earlier we noted that turnaround pastors are considered by some to be workaholics. Here is one reason why. They not only do everything their predecessors did but continually add to the church program.

Of course, no matter how positive the additions to ministry are, some will not be happy. Fine. Count the yes votes, not the no votes. Why should "no" votes count ten, and "yes" votes only one?

It makes little sense to allow a disgruntled minority to hold the church captive. Many church patriarchs have grown accustomed to simply shaking their head "no" and everything stopping dead in its tracks. No longer. Their participation is certainly welcomed, but the new exciting and biblical ministries will go on with or without them.

These initial steps towards change should not be radical, but biblical disciplines. The assumption: "Of course we will do these things, the Word instructs us to. If I need to do them on my own time after the machinery of the church has been oiled, fine. But I will be doing it. Those who wish to join me are welcome."

- Just do it!

- Do the right things alone, at first, if necessary.

- Don't be surprised that people in a dying church are complacent.

- Invite positive people to join you personally.

- Don't count the "no" votes, but the "yes" votes.

#2 Turnaround leaders accept responsibility for the turnaround.
This responsibility, however, means leading others to own vision.

"Bad goals are your goals. Good goals are our goals."

If a pastor is not prepared to accept responsibility, he should resign! Too many leaders confuse responsibility ("response able") with recognition and credit. When success follows, share the praise with others. Without a committed laity, nothing of lasting value will occur.

It is astounding how many "leaders" are too quick to receive the pat on the back for success, and run for cover when the charts turn south. Instead of owning the challenge they often shift the blame to staff, boards, or some nebulous "external" factor. How then does a pastor direct his lay-leadership in developing exciting goals?

A personal experience

When I arrived at our present church in Glendora, California, in 1991, I asked for attendance records, realizing that even the best intentioned memories are flawed. The natural tendency for long-time church members is to either exaggerate or diminish the past depending upon their personal experiences and relationship to a senior pastor during that representative period. I discovered the church had peaked in 1975. It had then declined sharply. In fact the chart formed a predictable bell curve.

For 15 years morning worship attendance fluctuated below the 800 ceiling.

My predecessor had begun several excellent steps to lay a foundation for health, such as the rewriting of an outdated constitution and initiating a contemporary service. Nonetheless Grace was definitely a plateaued church, the type Barna claims seldom finds new life.

The first order of business was to gather the existing leadership team and call for a two-day planning retreat. Approximately 25 men and women gathered. The staff began by presenting a detailed analysis of our current reality. Facts, charts, graphs and statistics from each of our major departments were presented.

I then encouraged them to dream. With eyes closed I invited them to picture what their church might look like in 10 years. No one was to worry about housekeeping. Whether we could afford it or the congregation would approve it were not to be considered. All they needed to do was ask, "What great things might our church do to glorify God?"

They were then divided into small groups of six by random selection. Their task was to return to the plenary group and report their conclusions. It was remarkable how similar the groups' visions were. I recorded their dreams. We looked for the consensus items in this master plan. In our case they believed God would have us remain at out present location. They arrived at a maximum number of morning worship attenders, and felt we would continue to hold multiple services. They also saw the Sunday school as a primary tool for group life.

The next day, we once again divided into small groups. The agenda was now for them to come back with no more than five one-year measurable goals which would move us toward this desired future for our church. I did not personally sit in any of the small groups.

Hours later they brought their reports. I once again recorded them. There was a wide variety of suggested goals, but we were able to find five specific consensus goals which we believed would move us closer to where we felt God wanted us to be. Grace was on its way to a new beginning. This process is repeated annually.

I have been using this basic planning concept for over 20 years. There are at least three benefits to this method of strategizing.

1) The leadership team knows the only unacceptable decision is doing nothing! If we always do what we've always done we will always get what we've always got. Not growing may be a reality. After all, ultimately fruitfulness is God's work. But not trying is not an option! It is the turn-around leader's responsibility to keep dreaming alive.

2) Though I do not participate in the small recommending groups, I have yet, in 20 years, to have the larger group insist upon a goal which they knew I did not support. Pastors do not (and should not) always get their way. They can usually prevent something from happening if they feel strongly enough it should not occur. Lay people know this. When they feel loved by their pastor and believe he has their best interest at heart, they want him on board.

3) Just because a program or ministry does not make the top five goals one year does not mean it cannot be done. The goal-setting process simply mandates what must be attempted, but it does not prevent other innovative endeavors from being carried out. Effective goal setting is a true win-win situation.

Understanding "consensus"

Responsible leaders must continually explain what is meant by "consensus." Perhaps the following story will be helpful.

Years ago after a day playing in the pool together my family decided we would go get something to eat and take it to a nearby park. We piled into the car happy and excited. Then I made a fatal mistake. I asked innocently "What would you like to eat?" I received four different opinions (I was neutral). My son wanted tacos, one daughter insisted on hamburgers, another chicken, and my wife was in the mood for fish. I made several compromise suggestions to no avail. No one seemed willing to compromise.

Perhaps it was plain orneriness on my part, but I declared, "You shall each have your wish. We'll go to Long John Silvers for fish, then to Taco Bell, to Kentucky Fried Chicken, and over to McDonalds. You will each hold your food until all have been served. We will then go to the park and eat our meal together."

Which is precisely what we did. Ludicrous — yes! It's been over eight years since that afternoon and I've yet to have the family be as stubborn as they were that day.

If we wish to do something *together* we must make a choice. We are not talking about compromise on moral or doctrinal issues. We agree on the direction and priorities. Our desire to be with one another outweighs our desire to have our own way.

No matter what fast food restaurant a car load of people selects, someone will be happiest and someone else the least happy about the choice. Consensus does not mean I'm ecstatic about every decision. Sometimes I am, other times I "am less so." Finding consensus means we trust one another. We enjoy being in a cooperative endeavor, knowing we can do more together than we can separately.

A leader *is responsible for helping those around him understand how childish it is to always insist on getting their way.* One way to do this is by maintaining a good attitude when decisions are not exactly your first choice. The direction is more important than the details. If we're heading in the right direction we'll eventually get where we want to be. Keeping the big picture in mind is essential.

Accept responsibility for raising the financial resources to accomplish the dreams

Surprising as it may seem, the larger the organization the smaller the decision making group needs to be. Also, the larger the church the smaller percentage of congregants needed to own a project or direction in order for it to be successful. For a full discussion of this you may wish to read *The Very Large Church* by Lyle Schaller, Nashville: Abingdon Press, 2000 (c.f. pp.152–155, 170).

It has been suggested the pastor should retain his role as spiritual leader and not the primary raiser of funds. The fallacy of this is both biblical and practical.

Jesus said, "Where your treasure is your heart shall be also" and elsewhere, "You cannot serve God and mammon." This implies that what we do with our money is a very spiritual matter. Where a church allocates its funds indicates its spiritual priorities.

I suspect many wish to distance themselves from the responsibility for raising funds as a subconscious means of buffering themselves from blame if failure results. Money follows God-directed goals as surely as water follows a downward terrain. A leader convinced God wishes the church to renew its vitality will be confident of God's supply as well. It is God's will to build His church.

Pragmatically, whoever accepts responsibility for raising the money is the leader of the organization. Though seldom discussed, most people in the church understand this intuitively.

Understanding the "authority of submission"

I have coined the phrase "authority of submission" after many years of contemplating this paradox. Those God uses to bring dead churches back to significant presence in the community are not arrogant. These leaders know the task is impossible without an unusual working of God. These men often wish God had directed them to other types of ministries. You find them to be almost self-deprecating in regards to their own giftedness and abilities. They are simply vessels available for the Master's service. They understand this better than most.

They have, nonetheless, been called by God for this endeavor. This calling is not as mysterious as one might think. Surely, circumstances have been a factor. Possibly they would speak of some irresistible compelling work of the Spirit or perhaps a Scripture verse brought to their attention at a time of decision making.

These no-nonsense leaders mostly will rely heavily on the tangible, duly recorded vote of congregation or appointment by their denominational officials. It is because of this they arrive with confidence the Lord has **them** in this place for this time to do a work which needs doing. Could someone else do the job better?

Quite possibly. But that no longer matters once they arrive. God sent **them** there for this time and they are determined to lead until **He** removes them.

This is the authority of submission: submission to the appropriate calling or appointing group or person and to fulfilling their responsibility as long as they pastor the church. Before long someone will step forward to challenge their call to lead. (See chapter 5.)

Turnaround leaders do not relish these challenges but they are seldom cowered by them. When the question is raised to why he is leading, his response may sound something such as:

George, you seem to be asking me why I am making so many decisions and have enacted the program and goals of the board without consulting with you. That is a legitimate question. Hopefully, I have not violated any Scriptural or constitutional guidelines. (See chapter 8.) If I have, then I apologize and will make appropriate corrections.

But it seems the issue we're dealing with goes deeper than that. Is your real question why I'm the leader in this church? The answer to that is quite simple. The congregation called me here with the required vote. They have asked me to lead. Now it's possible they have changed their minds and perhaps they would even wish for you to take my place.

There is only one way we can know that. The by-laws prescribe the manner in which you can call for a business meeting. You will be permitted to make a proposal then. If the congregation wishes for me to leave, then I will do so with dignity and quietly. I'm confident the Lord will show me His will for me at that time.

In the meantime I'm assuming they still desire for me to lead. I am doing so in submission to their will. If I'm going to be dismissed I would prefer it be because I am doing what I felt they called me to do rather than because I neglected to honor their desires.

Some pastors, when challenged, have made the mistake of either calling the meeting themselves, or tending their resignation in disgust or fear.

If someone is to be a turnaround leader, he will be challenged. The dynamics of a decaying church are simply too convoluted for it to be any other way. Why bail out? Relatively few churches actually vote their pastors out by a majority vote. Usually the vociferous and vocal few intimidate him into leaving.

On a side note, it may not hurt to have your denominational leader give you a promise of backing prior to accepting the call to a historically troubled church. If these leaders are naive enough to think the turnaround can be done without bloodshed, they simply should not be in that position.

My dream, and it is probably only that, is that more denominations would send qualified leaders into deathbed situations with a commitment to support them financially if needed for at least three years.

#3 Turnaround leaders avoid a church which does not desire to become healthy.

The more issues a couple agrees on prior to the wedding ceremony, the greater the likelihood of a happy lifetime together. Just as a mature husband should not enter into the commitment of matrimony lightly, neither should a pastor go into a church blind or with a frivolous attitude.

He should ask hard questions and not permit the pulpit committee to brush lightly over the matter of their decline. Is the church prepared for change? Do they have a history of pastor-abuse? If so, what rationale and evidence can they bring to the table to assure him the next pastor will be treated any differently?

Many wives bounce from one abusive marriage into another. Why? They have a neurotic need to be taken advantage of. They have personal issues unresolved. Likewise any pastor who dances from one disaster to another should take a long look inside himself. Counsel may be in order when masochistic tendencies are evident.

There are hurting churches in America that sincerely long to be restored and will accept help from their shepherd. The secret is to discover those churches. To the casual observer they may appear much like the larger number of steadily declining gatherings on a sure path to extinction.

A - Z Discernment comes by careful thought

Some things to consider before accepting a call to be pastor:

A. Do they have a heartfelt desire for someone to lead them? Is this at the top of their list in their pastoral profile?

B. Was the cause of their decline a combination of dynamics which can be changed? (such as the death of a well-loved pastor, a moral failure, etc.)

C. Do they appear to be genuinely repentant for past neglect and failure, or are they still smug and proud? Is there brokenness?

D. Without prompting, do they admit they are on the edge? Do they have a realistic appraisal of their condition?

E. Is the location one which permits vigorous life? Is there room for parking expansion?

F. Are you the right color to lead this group of people?

G. How large is their debt compared to their annual receipts?

H. Do you enjoy spending time with members of the board and pulpit committee? Are they your type of people?

I. Are they "hungry" for you to come, or do they give the impression they are doing you a favor? Frankly the arrogance with which many churches approach pastoral candidates today is appalling. If you are happily involved in ministry, you should not be required to "apply" for the turnaround church. They should be courting you! (Note: I told my daughters never to chase after a boy or call him. Not bad advice for turnaround leaders.)

J. Are there one or two families carrying more than 30 percent of the church budget? What solid reason do you have to believe their financial deep pockets will allow you to lead?

K. Why isn't the previous pastor still there? What reasons do they give?

L. Are they seeking the twin or the opposite of the previous pastor? What does that tell you? Do you feel good about the message being sent?

M. How does your wife feel?

N. When you ask probing questions concerning the present plight of the church do you receive consistent answers?

O. Who are the key functional players and what good reason can you find to assume they will be on your team?

P. Are they requiring you to retain all existing staff?

Q. Are they offering a salary which demonstrates respect and a strong desire to have you come?

R. Are there any mixed messages? If so, have you confronted them? What response did you receive?

S. When you saw the pastor's study did it reveal respect for the office?

T. What does the predecessor have to say? Does it match what you were told by the pulpit committee?

U. Does your denominational executive encourage you to take this position?

V. Why are you open to moving? What opportunities for meaningful ministry does this church offer that you cannot find where you are presently?

W. Do you really trust the people you're talking to?

X. What's your motive in accepting this position?

Y. What reasons have been given by the pulpit committee for deciding you are the right person for the task? Are they valid? Well thought out? Or have they simply taken the recommendation of one or two people?

Z. Are you ready to commit at least seven years to this ministry?

#4 Turnaround leaders establish the critical rules of engagement before they arrive.

The time to negotiate is prior to arriving. A capable pastor will garner the respect of his best lay leaders by asking probing and thought provoking questions in the process of candidating. If he is considering leaving a productive place of service, move his family, and begin a new life, certainly the search committee knows a wise person will do this only after considering as many factors as possible contributing to his potential success.

While there may be many factors exacerbating the congregation's demise, there are usually one or two patterns or habits which head the list. The incoming pastor's ability to diagnose the predominant issues will give him credibility among his new parishioners. This demonstration of insight will give them hope he can do for them what they have been unable to do on their own.

To articulate his suspicions and observations prior to accepting the call also helps to depersonalize these matters. He has not been personally hurt by anyone. He is not picking on them. He has no axe to grind. I believe he should graciously and gently lay out what he perceives may be the problems of the past.

Then he may say, "Obviously those who have served before have been unable to solve these issues. I am only a man. I have limitations and feelings. I have no desire to come here and perpetuate recent history. I also do not wish to move my family knowingly so they can be hurt and you be disappointed. If you call me, this is what you will be voting for. If I agree to come be your pastor I will assume your vote to call is also a vote for the following…" He can then lay out specifically what the expectations are.

Illustrations of pastoral prenuptial agreements

Calvary Church

Calvary Church was located in a small town in the Eastern states. For decades its morning worship attendance fluctuated between 170 and 200. It experienced a devastating church split. The group that left warned, "We'll be back to pick up the pieces when you close the doors." Calvary's numbers dropped below 140.

The pastoral search committee looked for one year. Those they wished to attract would not consider the troubled church. Finally they extended a call to a young seminary graduate, Anthony, whom they had heard months earlier as a pulpit supply.

Twenty-nine-year-old Anthony came with little experience. He and his wife had three preschoolers. The salary offered was a barely livable wage ($20,000), health benefits and a parsonage with utilities paid. This pastor asked if they might consider reimbursing his mileage expenses and consider redecorating the 50-year-old parsonage.

After a lengthy trustee meeting, the lay leaders agreed to pour a new basement floor, install new carpet, add some paneling and apply a fresh coat of paint. That was all the negotiations.

Result: four years later attendance peaked at 340 following a building program.

Anthony asked for nothing more. Why? He knew he had nothing to bargain with. He had completed his seminary and was looking for a church to give him a chance to serve. His resume was not impressive nor had he proven any capabilities at that point of his career. All he asked for was an opportunity to grow, serve, and develop. If he had leadership capabilities, he knew they would validate themselves in time.

Bridgewood Community Church

Bridgewood Community Church had a 100-plus year history. It was located in the suburbs of a large Midwestern city. It had reached 300 in morning worship attendance 10 years previously but plateaued during the last decade.

It extended a call to Mike, who served a sister church in a neighboring state. Mike was being wooed by numerous churches that had heard of his achievements. He asked for a copy of Bridgewood's constitution and by-laws. Search committee members flew out to hear him preach and were impressed. They then invited him to fly out to meet with them.

Mike was impressed with the buildings and campus but was greatly concerned by the recent rewrite of the constitution. It appeared the church had made amendments to prevent a pastor from "taking too much control." When they called and invited him to candidate he told them he was probably not the man for whom they were looking.

The national director of the church's denomination called the pastor and asked why he had declined. He responded, "Their constitution excludes the pastor from both the nominating and budget committees. Billy Graham could not lead them according to that structure. It is like a wife saying to her husband, 'Honey, I love you and wish for you to lead our home, but you have nothing to say about the children or our money.'" The director suggested he tell the church why he had declined because other capable leaders would likely have similar concerns.

When they called again he explained their concerns. They admitted they had reacted to a controlling pastor and, if he would consider candidating, the board and pulpit committee would promise to take those restrictions from the constitution.

Knowing it was a risk, and fearing the church did not actually seek a true leader, the pastor agreed to come. True to their word the amendments were presented at the first business meeting upon his arrival. The congregation supported them.

Result: Over six years the church did achieve its historic high attendance, but the fundamental control issues were never resolved and a decade later the church still averages between 250 and 300.

First Church of Garden Grove

First Church of Garden Grove had long been a flagship church for its denomination. During its peak years it had reaped a great harvest when its California community transformed from orange trees to wall-to-wall houses. Under the direction of a personality pastor it topped 1000 for one year. Then internal struggles encouraged the pastor to resign and it settled into a comfortable plateau, averaging between 700 and 800 in its morning services. While many churches around First Church were becoming mega-churches, some members at First were quite content with their comfortable size. A few recalled the glory days and longed to re-enact them.

The search committee at First Church received word of a middle-aged pastor who appeared to have a credible track record in turnaround ministries. They knew their number one priority in a pastor must be leadership. The church could not move ahead without strong direction.

The pastor in whom they were interested was comfortably settled in his present ministry. Rick had fought the wars, built a house, and was not anxious to leave. The committee, however, felt confident this man was the one for them.

After protracted interaction, Rick agreed to come candidate if two issues could be resolved. First, the board would remove all expectations for member care from his shoulders. He knew his gifts were not in the area of compassion and counsel. He also realized that to move a church from 700 would be impossible if the members were expecting him personally to visit them in the hospital and do shut-in calls. Second, he requested he be given unilateral authority over the church staff including, but not limited to, the authority to hire and fire.

He requested that not only should the board place these agreements in their minutes at the beginning of each year but also the body would know when they voted to call him they were agreeing to these tenets.

Result: The church called him to come though many of the staff families and close friends voted "no." In the next years the church enjoyed close to 50 percent growth, and is establishing historic high attendance.

These illustrations will hopefully help you as you contemplate what key changes must take place for the church you are considering accepting to resurrect itself and become all God may wish it to be. Do you have the "chips" to negotiate those changes?

Summary

This chapter outlines the first four characteristics of turnaround leaders. First, they consider leadership as an act of service. They do not ask for permission to lead, but lead wisely, building consensus as they move along. Doing nothing, however, is not an option. Early wins are a must. They keep the church focused on the main thing. These leaders accept the burden for changing the course of the church. They build coalitions but know ultimately the responsibility for raising necessary resources is theirs. They model submission. They understand that their right to lead will be challenged but refuse to quit or become detoured when it is. Turnaround pastors scrutinize a church carefully before accepting a call. They are especially tuned in to their church's receptivity to leadership. Finally, turnaround leaders negotiate dynamics and agreements essential for success prior to arrival.

CHAPTER 8

Characteristics of Turnaround Leaders (continued)

#5 Turnaround leaders never backtrack.

There can be no progress without change. In their book *Blur: The Speed of Change in the Connected Economy* (Addison-Wesley, 1998, p.13), Stan Davis and Christopher Meyer conclude, "Built to last now means built to change." The leader must accept this before he can begin to prepare his key players for what lies ahead.

My friend Jay Pankratz led a church from 400 to over 2000. In his excellent seminar, "Turnaround Church" Jay suggests a number of things in such a church that probably need changing:

- ◆ From decline to growth

- ◆ From maintenance to outreach

- ◆ From traditional to contemporary music

- ◆ From one/two services to three or four

- ◆ From an old name to a new name

- ◆ From old facilities to new/improved facilities

- ◆ From one site to an additional satellite church site

- ◆ From borrowing to no debt

- From ethnic homogeneity to ethnic diversity

- From current staff to new staff

- From a cumbersome constitution to a streamlined constitution

- From multi-boards to one board

- From lecture classes to small groups

And I might add a few more:

- From committees to teams or task forces

- From pastor as caregiver to pastor as leader

- From a board of "nay-sayers" to permission givers

- From a past focus to a future focus

Your church may not need, nor choose, to make all these changes. But if no changes were needed your predecessor would probably still be there and you would be unnecessary.

Change always brings some degree of conflict

Recognizing the need for change points out that the current situation isn't working. Accepting this will naturally be difficult because:

- No matter how graciously the change is presented it does convey that what someone (or some groups) has been doing is not adequate. They will take this personally unless they are unusual individuals or have participated in the decision-making process.

- Most people don't mind change they just don't want you to change them. For example most people will accept a new worship style or service time as long as no attempt is made to reconstruct or reschedule their service of choice. We are all creatures of habit.

- None of us like to be acted upon. It brings out our victim's role.

- The glue that holds many congregations together is the "glue of growing old together." Conversations float, like water running downhill, toward the way things used to be. This is especially difficult if the ways things used to be in the church were actually better than they are today. The defense mechanism for resisting change is to believe the church can go back to doing things the way it was done back when old pastor "whatever-his-name" did it. The fact that society has changed is missed or denied totally. Someone commented, "It is fine to preach Spurgeon's sermons if you have Spurgeon's audience." Otherwise it is time to move into the new millennium.

- The premise that the church is first a spiritual institution. "Jesus Christ is the same yesterday, today, and forever" (Hebrews 13:8). Too many illogically assume that means methodology within the church is more Christlike the less it changes. This may be overcome to some degree by continually emphasizing your orthodoxy.

- Change always entails bringing new lay leadership into the loop. This threatens those who have sacrificed finances, time and energy to maintain the church for years. They are made to feel incompetent, inadequate, old, and unimportant. They sense replacement is inevitable.

- Declining churches are often run by members who have been together for decades. The new pastor has yet to prove his character and competency. Why should they accept the radical suggestions of an unknown?

The emotions of being out of control

My family was driving an all-nighter from Seattle down to southern California when we heard a loud knocking coming from the right rear wheel of the van. I asked my wife to stop, and I got out to look in the dark. At first I found nothing. After further inspection, however, I noticed that four of the five lugs holding the tire on the wheel were completely shorn off. We had one lug securing our tire as we drove down the southern slope of Mount Shasta at 75 miles per hour.

Of course we needed to call for a tow. We were in a desolate stretch (miles from the nearest exit). It was almost 1 a.m. In time, a marine heading back to his base stopped and offered to go to the next exit and call for a tow. We sat for another hour wondering if he had kept his word. Eventually a tow truck arrived.

At first we were thrilled. We needed help and it had arrived. Out of the truck a sleepy young man, about 18 or 19 years of age. He walked around to survey our situation, then with little explanation shoved a piece of paper under my nose and asked me to sign it. He then said, "Your family can stay in the car."

He returned to his truck, turned it around facing the wrong way on the freeway, lifted the back end of our van off the ground, and before I knew it I was experiencing one of the most helpless feelings in my life heading down the freeway at 65 miles per hour backwards at 2:30 in the morning. There I was attached to a tow truck being driven by a kid almost young enough to be my son, going to an unknown location with the most precious cargo I had, my family, with no way to tell him to slow down or check the hook-up on our car.

I suspect many people have similar feelings when a strong turnaround pastor begins to pull them to where they need to go. We gain trust from our people by demonstrating character, competency, capacity, and content. We cannot, however, afford to spend a decade winning trust. The car must be moved off the freeway. If they call the pastor, they must trust him to take them to safety and repairs.

So far we've suggested change is necessary and change will create some level of discomfort and conflict. Therefore when it is time for the turn-around leader to step over the comfort line and implement well thought-out changes, he needs to be prepared for confrontation and intimidation. Too often a leader announces what he is planning to do and then pulls back when opposed. Unless there is new information brought to the table he should not back down. The threat of some being upset and others leaving should not be considered new information.

Four keys to avoid having to backtrack

When a pastor backtracks after announcing a new direction, he loses the respect of those who are prepared to follow his leadership. When a pastor says, "Let's go" but retracts each time opposition surfaces he demoralizes his loyalists. Preparation and resolution can prevent this, however.

1) Know your Bible!

Recognizing Christ's mandates to churches can give the pastor the confidence to move forward in a number of areas:

- win the lost to Jesus Christ

- spend quality and quantity time in the Word

- disciple those who come to faith

- encourage loving relationships

- confront sin according to Matthew 18

- preach against sin and for righteousness

- make his family a high priority

- use his time wisely (See appendix at end of book.)

- be a steward of his resources

- refuse to become consumed with "empty chatter"

- avoid gossip

- refuse to show partiality

- welcome new people into the church

- baptize those who believe

- be kind to everyone

When a pastor requests permission for these things, he demeans his calling and unwittingly diminishes his standing before the flock.

When the Bible is clear, it makes no difference what others may think about his actions. He must be willing to deny himself, take up his cross and follow Jesus. If his congregation fires him, so be it. He has no choice if he is to remain obedient to the One who called him.

Ted Engstrom, in his wonderful book, *Your Gift of Administration* (Nashville: Thomas Nelson Publishers, 1983), reminds leaders they are not responsible for how others feel about their work; they are responsible to do what is right. Not all decisions are worth dying for. The responsibilities listed above are. To refuse to do them out of cowardice is tantamount to the sin of Baalam, who was a prophet to the highest bidder.

2) Know your by-laws

Long before candidating the pastor should have made a thorough study of these documents. When he accepts his position he has agreed to abide by them unless previous contractual arrangements have been made to amend them.

These by-laws may sometimes be cumbersome, but they are all that stands between the church and anarchy. They represent a legal document. Work within them. In most cases they become the pastor's friend! The by-laws usually have built in safeguards against abusive behavior by cantankerous members.

Never should a leader embark upon a plan of action without first consulting the by-laws to see whether he can remain within the spirit of them and carry out the plan.

Do not carry the constitution with you and continually refer to it. Doing so will create a climate of pharisaism. Before long you'll find yourself surrounded by a group of wanna-be lawyers. Put it in a desk drawer. Examine it in private. If something cannot be done, you want to know that. Act accordingly. If changes can be made legally, move ahead. Only when a significant challenge is brought against a proposal do you casually explain that the by-laws permit it and you'll be implementing it. This will generate calls from church members to the office requesting copies of the by-laws. Have them ready. Also expect them to be read with a fine-tooth comb. Everything else you're doing had best be according to the document as well.

I've discovered that in churches with long histories, culture slowly begins to supplant the actual constitution. If you are new to the church, you may have a golden opportunity to reinstitute changes, which in actuality are more in keeping with the written document than the manner in which the church has been functioning.

For example, when I arrived at our present church, I discovered a delight-fully streamlined constitution and by-laws. I have thanked my prede-cessor for his sacrificial efforts in this regard. However, I noted that the senior pastor was designated as "presiding elder" but had not been chairing either congregational or board meetings. Some pastors prefer not to. I've discovered many thorny issues can be avoided by wise handling of group discussions. As I am likely to be the one most accus-tomed to thinking on his feet, comfortable in front of a group, and familiar with the details of the church, I prefer to moderate board and congregational meetings. I felt it was important to establish my role as chair from the first board meeting.

One week before our first elder meeting I called the "president of the board" (which our by-laws refers to as the corporate officer to sign legal documents) to arrange a breakfast meeting. I asked him to come with any items he felt needed to be brought to the board. The morning we met we combined our lists. An agreement was made that while he and I did not need to agree on every issue, we would have a pact of "no surprises." I then prepared a board agenda. Each board agenda has three sections:

Information Items: This is a long list of programs, updates, and staff matters I believe the board would like to know about. The goal is to keep them "in the know."

Discussion Items: Usually two or three matters of substance such as policies, strategies or directional matters, about which I have not made up my mind and sincerely desire to reap the benefits of collective counsel. The goal is to discuss whether it is a good idea and, if so, what modifications are necessary.

Decision Items: In 10 years we have always found consensus on these, primarily because when I discover opposition at the discussion level it never comes to the board for a vote.

At our first elder meeting I passed out the agenda and commented in an assumptive manner, "I noticed in your by-laws that the pastor is the presiding officer. I did look that up in the dictionary, and I guess that means I'm to guide our meetings. The first item of business is..." Though previous pastors had chosen to allow laymen to preside, we have been doing it differently since my arrival.

At the first congregational meeting I simply assumed I'd chair it. The real issue here is not whether you chair the board or congregational meetings. The point is that pastors need not be fearful of implementing whatever the constitution and by-laws permit.

One final comment on this touchy issue. What if the governing document you inherited is prohibitive to growth? What if it calls for too many committees, grants no authority to the pastor, or requires business meetings for virtually all expenditures and salary discussions? Move toward an amendment if you must but read carefully the next section!

3) Know your backing

Recently a number of writers on church growth have adopted the metaphor of "pastoral poker." I personally resist that for a couple of reasons. One, there is no "luck of the draw" in turnaround leadership. We are dealing with the sovereign work of God. God loves the church, has given His Son for the church and will not leave anything to chance. He providentially directs his leaders to a place of service and will by His Spirit direct the same in bringing about healthy change. Two, I am too cheap to gamble so have limited exposure to poker.

Let's substitute a chess metaphor. It is preferred because there is no luck involved. The player has complete control over his moves. He is given time to ponder carefully the options and implications of each move. It is a game of skill and experience. The variables are chosen strategy and the opponent's maneuvers. The player must know his objectives and adjust according to the reality of the other's moves. The most skilled player wins.

In every chess game there are critical junctures when a player is forced to evaluate his positional strength. Should he make a trade? Sacrifice a piece? Opt for a power move (moving the queen)? What is the worst that could happen if a move is made, and could he survive it if he does?

There are times when the wise strategy is a solid defense and retrenchment. Other times retreat spells disaster. Maybe the time has come to push for checkmate.

How much relative strength do you currently have? If the conflict escalates to a vote of the board, will you carry the vote? If a congregational meeting is called, will you have the required percentage of votes to survive? Who are your votes? Are your supporters able to financially underwrite the church program should the disenfranchised opt to withhold or redirect their giving?

Money is always the last thing to arrive and the first to go. In seasons of change, a leader must assume funds will be withheld by those who oppose it. The calculation should be figured into the equation early. If you chart your annual giving you may wish to force the change issue at times of peak giving. This will not alter the annual giving total but may provide a few months to adjust the budget until new growth arrives.

I have discovered that often when a church moves boldly ahead, some people with significant financial resources step up to the plate. At one of the darkest moments in our pastoral career we had broken the back of stubborn opposition. Yet the bills needed to be paid. It was New Year's Eve. Following the service a couple who had been marginally involved asked it they could take my family to dinner. I agreed, just glad to be with friendly faces. As dinner ended and we walked to the parking lot Will handed me two envelopes and asked if the church could deposit these gifts in the old calendar year. I told him I would see to it, and placed them in my coat pocket. I didn't even bother to look at them until the next day. Inside were two checks: one from this family and another from a relative. To my knowledge, they were the two largest checks that church had received.

A week later I called to express thanks on behalf of the church. He said, "We've been in this church for decades. We've wondered why pastors put up with the mean-spirited attitudes. We're grateful you are at least willing to try to change things."

At that point I knew we had the financial backing to move forward with turnaround changes.

The backing to be considered is not always financial. Often it involves influence. People, especially in smaller churches, tend to vote in blocks. Each group has one or two opinion setters. Rather than lobby the group as a whole, which usually smacks of politics at its worst, it is better to develop a trusting relationship with the gatekeepers to the group. When they can be persuaded, change takes place more simply. Let them own the change when possible and sell it for you.

How many chess pieces do you have on the board? Are they positioned where needed? If not, quietly move them into position before a show-down. If you see you cannot win a frontal assault, establish a good pawn defense.

Turnaround pastors realize they may gain backing through the little things. They refuse to allow challenges to paralyze them into nonaction. They work hard, do the right things, preach to the best of their ability, love the people, and wait. Time and patience may be your ally.

Dr. Wally Criswell of the famed First Baptist Church of Dallas, Texas, tells this story. He followed a legacy, George Truett. In those days the success of a church was primarily evaluated by its Sunday school attendance. Many who remained loyal to Pastor Truett did not want Dr. Criswell to succeed. They continually referred to the "grand old days" and claimed the new pastor's effectiveness was dwarfed by comparison.

Dr. Criswell sensed the church was progressing nicely so he went to the Sunday school superintendent and asked to see the Sunday school records. His request was denied. He was told that was none of his business; others were assigned to be the keepers of these records (those loyal to Truett).

He understood how things work in a church. He went back to preaching and leading. He waited several years. On his anniversary Sunday (big deal in old Southern Baptist churches), he invited all those who had joined the church during his tenure as pastor to stand. He noted more stood than were remaining seated.

The next day he approached the Sunday school superintendent once again and asked to see the records. They were handed to him.

The principle is simple. Don't force an issue you cannot win. Waiting on nonessential issues may be the better part of valor.

4) *Know your "Bob"* (Robert's Rules of Order)

Unless your constitution states otherwise, a congregational meeting will probably be run according to Robert's Rules of Order. Ideally it will sit on your shelf and gather dust.

Most pastors I know view this aged guidebook for parliamentary procedures with disdain. Since turnaround churches are more likely than not to have at least one ugly public meeting, you probably should blow the dust off and familiarize yourself with its content. It can be your friend.

The underlying purpose of Robert's Rules is to assure fairness and decorum in emotionally charged public debate. At its best this can assist the church body in doing its business decently and in order.

Ideally you'll never need it

Please do not misunderstand. In our present church we have only one business meeting per year with any real business to conduct. We vote on our budget and affirm our elders. The budget passes by voice vote with virtually no questions and the elder ratification has been essentially unanimous (done by private ballot) due to the quality of men with which we have been blessed. These meetings are more of a celebration than a business meeting.

But it is not always this way. A church must grow into such a culture and earn the trust of its people by good management and a track record of dependable leadership.

When do we need Bob?

- ◆ Robert's Rules may need to be invoked when a church is undergoing an overt division.

- ◆ Robert's Rules may need to be used when church members have a long history of standing in public business sessions and shouting out to one another.

- ◆ Robert's Rules will be necessary when one, two, or three dominant persons speak pontifically to every comment.

- ◆ Robert's Rules are helpful when the issue on the floor is particularly emotionally charged.

- ◆ Robert's Rules will be essential when the threat of a lawsuit is present.

When the congregation appears evenly split

Robert's Rules assure that both sides of an issue receive equal time. The role of the chair is to permit both viewpoints to be heard. A motion should be on the floor prior to any discussion. At that time members (only) are instructed to stand, address the chair (not one another), and state whether they will be speaking in favor of the motion or against it. Then they do so.

A good chairperson will suggest a time limit for each person who speaks. After everyone who wishes to speak has opportunity, a person may speak a second time if he or she is granted permission by vote of those present. The speeches may only address the motion on the floor and should never attack another person.

Any alteration in the motion requires a vote to amend and a majority vote to support the amendment. Idle chatter is discouraged.

It sometimes helps congregations to know these rules prior to beginning. I have at times pointed out that the vote will be done by private ballot (if that is the case) and that anyone speaking to the issues will forfeit the benefit of confidential voting. I also point out if everyone in the room feels the need for three minutes, we will be there a long time.

A meeting run according to Robert's Rules tends to take the "fun" out of it for many people who simply like to hear themselves talk or love to argue. The intended function of a business meeting is to allow people within the church to retain veto power on major issues, not to affect policy and micromanage the organization.

Some, however, feel their service and giving obligates them to help formulate every decision in their church. A friend observed, "Just because I buy a ticket does not mean I have the right to fly the plane."

My personal conviction is that a business meeting is the absolutely worst place to do business. If we must vote, let's do it and get on with our lives.

A helpful note about Robert's Rules

Buried in Robert's Rules is the little comment: "The suggestion of the chair carries the order of the day unless challenged." This is one of the reasons I prefer to moderate meetings. The purpose is not to be heavy-handed or manipulative. Some issues before the assembly are of such magnitude it behooves the congregation to be fully informed, and time for healthy discussion is important if for no other reason than for the leadership to hear where the people stand and to know what perceptions must be corrected and how much communication is necessary to move a major initiative ahead. A building project is one obvious example.

Other issues are perfunctory and all reasonable members recognize it. Why waste time with needless discussion which too often becomes an open floor for airing issues better handled one on one?

The moderator can suggest a voice vote or ballot vote. It is his call, unless the constitution states otherwise. He can ask for a vote of consensus. He can call for a moment of prayer. He can request permission to table a matter until further study is done. He can suggest time limits for discussion. All is permissible unless one person speaks to challenge his suggestion. However the moment a member objects, the discussion must revert to a more formal following of the restrictive Robert's Rules.

Feel free to agree or disagree

Possibly this discussion concerning "Bob" is irrelevant in your situation. My purpose is solely to present it as another tool for consideration in the most difficult moments of enacting change.

#6 Turnaround leaders keep close reign on their temper.

Effective leaders live in the power of the Holy Spirit as a habit of life. They manifest the fruit of the Spirit. Temper tantrums spell disaster. Leaders will be challenged, tested, provoked, opposed, lied about, misrepresented, despised, and probably encounter hostile conspiracies. Bottom line: If you can't stand the heat in the kitchen get out. With heat comes pressure. With pressure is the tendency to explode.

There are a number of reasons the turnaround leader needs to make this a matter of perpetual prayer.

- ◆ Loss of temper is sin (Ephesians 4:26; Psalm 4:4; Proverbs 12:16; 14:17; 15:1; 19:11; 22:24-25; 25:28).

- ◆ Displays of temper are usually a public act.

- ◆ By definition losing one's temper implies loss of self-control. Self-control is a fruit of the Spirit's control. So, by losing our temper we publicly display we have, at least for the moment, functioned outside the control of God's Spirit.

- ◆ Our leadership diminishes in credibility. After all, the turnaround strategy presented has supposedly been bathed in prayer, based on the Word, and is free from self-centered motives.

Practical ideas to keep from bursting

1) Depersonalize opposition.

As I mentioned previously, I have a quote hanging in my office that I see several times a day: "People are not really against you, they are merely for themselves." In the daily fare of life this is true. Your determination to re-engineer church life interrupts members' comfort zones. It is not you they resist but what you represent: change; high expectations; impending competition from new, more committed members; reminders of their personal spiritual failure in the past; etc.

If you have tackled the monstrous task of leading the charge for new health, you are the logical lightning rod. If it weren't you, it would be someone else.

2) In cases of frontal assaults upon your leadership by a recalcitrant group, remember the "glue of the common enemy."

In some combative situations people will actually attack you verbally. Once again you can depersonalize the attack by recognizing that these members have probably found a unity because of their common wish to rid the church of your leadership. They do not dislike you as a person but detest what you are trying to do to their church. In most cases, as soon as the issue is resolved, their coalition will disappear. The one exception is when family ties exist. Blood is thicker than water. It's probably best to accept that a family will act as a unit. Stop trying to fight it. Move on.

You also need to consider the source of the criticism. I once had a woman approach me with tearful eyes and say, "I just don't get it, Pastor. I've had four pastors and have had problems with every one of them." She honestly did not get it. The problem was not that the Lord had sent her four loser pastors. What are the statistical odds of that? The problem was her. Love those people but do not allow them to dominate your emotions.

3) Deflect the arrows when appropriate.

If the current philosophies, directions, priorities, and programs of the church have been owned by the duly chosen board and leaders, it is permissible to let unhappy members know that. You can say, "This is not solely my decision. If you are upset you need to express your feelings to the group. I have been unable to help you so the next step is for me to arrange a meeting with the executive board."

Once you have patiently attempted to work with the disenfranchised, it is not weak leadership to allow the team to help. By going to the board (if they signed off on what is taking place—and hopefully they did) the results will be positive.

If they are committed to the new direction and genuinely seek new life for the church the board will tell the member so. By insisting they go to the board, you prevent the divide and conquer maneuver which members have proven works so well in the past. That is, they get on the phone or corner each board member one-on-one. Many board members are more anxious to be nice than effective so they offer promises to the member to get them off their back. This is more difficult when the entire board meets as a unit.

By offering to have chronic complainers meet with the board you show respect for the board. They are viewed as a valued contributing part of the process of change. They will be seen not merely as yes men. The congregation will realize they are dealing not with one lonely individual but a group. This is part of building a successful bandwagon.

What if the board is intimidated and gets cold feet? As tragic as this may be, at least you know better where you stand at the moment. It may be time to develop new board members.

4) Find healthy outlets for pent up emotions.

In periods of constant attack a leader simply cannot afford not to exercise. This is not only essential for energy, but it provides a source of transference. Play basketball, run, do push-ups, hike, jet ski, or golf. Some pastors find it therapeutic to write first names on their golf balls.

5) Make good friends.

There is nothing like being able to talk through difficulties with a trusted companion. But be careful. Keep reading.

#7 Turnaround leaders are discreet about what they share with others.

James 1:19 cautions us to be slow to speak and more ready to listen. Unfortunately many otherwise competent pastors reverse it. I guess since they feel called to preach and like to talk they assume they should talk all the time. An old military expression is an excellent reminder for pastors: "Loose lips sink ships."

It is especially important to exercise extreme caution at the beginning of a pastorate. In two of my three pastorates, the chairman of the pulpit committee left shortly after I took over. In both cases I know they felt betrayed because I did not make them my confidant and elevate them to the second most influential position in any church, "pastor's right-hand man."

It is necessary for every pastor to have personal counsel. I find it disconcerting, however, when anyone strives to appoint themselves to that position.

The search committee members and board members in place when a pastor is called often have hidden agendas. Perhaps they secretly wish to perpetuate the status quo or hope the new pastor will finally deal with someone in the body with whom they have been at odds for years. Maybe they wish to sing more often or become chairman of the board.

Not everyone in a church has a negative agenda, but most everyone has some agenda. The pastor must be especially careful until he is able to ferret these out.

Shortly after arriving at the church, the pastor will hear something like this: "Pastor, I realize your job is a lonely one. There are so many expectations, and everyone expects you to act perfect. I want you to feel like you can just be yourself when we're together."

When I hear these words, several questions pop into mind. Do I look lonely? Just exactly what is it I'm supposed to do when we're together? Get drunk? Watch a racy movie? Scratch myself in some hard to reach spot? Burp? And why would I wish to do these things at all, or with him? Is he telling me he will never view me as more than another guy, that I will never be permitted to become the bishop of his soul?

A pastor is on all the time whether he likes it or not. His calling is a calling, not an eight-hour job.

Can you picture yourself driving home from a basketball game with one of the law enforcement officers in your congregation, parking in front of a 7-11 and asking him, "Hey buddy, you're off duty aren't you? Good, because I'm going to hold this place up at gunpoint."

Choose friends carefully. Turnaround leaders never lose sight of what they came to do. They probably had friends where they came from and hope to create close trusting and intimate relationships in their new church.

But caution is needed. Only time will reveal who stays on board. In the meantime anything you say can and may be used against you.

When entering a troubled church it is wise to initially process your thinking with someone outside the congregation. Over time trusted friendships will evolve. Until then be discreet.

8 Turnaround leaders are willing to confront the sin of divisiveness.

> "Reject a factious man after a first and second warning knowing that such a man is perverted and is sinning, being self-condemned" (Titus 3:10-11).

Few sins are tolerated in most churches as often as the sin of a contentious, disruptive and divisive person. William Easum wrote an article titled " On Not Being Nice For the Sake of the Gospel" (Net Results, April 1997). I later read he received more positive response from that article than anything he had ever published. The reason is not hard to figure out. He put his finger on an issue which has been too long ignored.

> Throughout my consulting ministry, I have seen a disturbing pattern: Most established churches are held hostage by bullies. Some individual or small group...opposes the church's making any radical change, even if it means the change would give the church a chance to thrive again. Courageous pastors often ask, "What do I do when one or two persons intimidate the church so much that it is not willing to try something new?" My response is always, "Either convert them, neutralize them, kick them out, or kill them. The Body cannot live with cancer. . . .

Easum says the willingness to deal with obstructionistic people is an act of love. He reminds his readers that Jesus loved enough to confront when he saw others held in bondage by the religious authorities of His day. He continues:

> Almost every struggling church has at least one dysfunctional bully who goes out of the way to be a big fish in a small pond. Often that is the primary reason the church is strug-gling. This person gets a sense of self-worth by keeping the church so intimidated, either by actions or money, that very

little can happen without the person's approval. The sad thing is that most of the leaders know this person presents a stumbling block to the church's future but will not do anything about it . . .

Easum is absolutely on target. Because we have dealt with this aggressive bully in chapter five we need not spend more time here.

Let's focus on the bully who is more subtle, elusive and prevalent: That person who undermines the growth of a church by a continual stream of derogatory remarks, criticisms, barbed questions, and insinuation.

Be on the alert for the Absalom warning signs

When King David was preoccupied with the overwhelming task of solidifying the kingdom, building its cities, and exterminating the enemies, his son sat daily in the gate. Scriptures do not tell us Absalom had any real responsibilities. He contributed nothing to the cause of the kingdom. He sat in the gate daily listening to the complaints of the people. Many were unhappy because David did not have time to hear their issues. But, of course David was busy running the country.

Absalom seized the moment. He reinforced the validity of the people's complaints and concerns and added, "If I were king I would deal with your concerns."

No, he wouldn't. If Absalom had been king he would have been busy working instead of sitting in the gate listening to people's sad stories.

A divisive person is often hard to pin down because he presents the persona of a compassionate listening ear. How can one criticize that?

In time he positions himself as a magnet for discontent. Word gets out that this individual is a sensitive and understanding confidant, especially if complaints involve the pastor's faults and where the church is currently heading. Call him or her if you were not visited. Talk to him or her if the sound system is too loud. Write him or her if you have been wounded in any manner.

Taking on the cause of the people

In time Absalom showed his true colors. He revolted. He positioned himself as the champion of the downtrodden, neglected people in David's kingdom.

When a divisive person decides it's time to voice "concerns" he usually begins by saying, "A number of people have come to me . . ." This is intended to give him leverage because he is first trusted by the people, and second speaks for many. It also makes him hard to pin down.

Force them to declare themselves early

Turnaround leaders tend to be blunt. Ask point-blank, "Do these people's sentiments represent your own?" The sin of division is virtually impossible to deal with if it is not brought out in the open.

In this open conversation elicit a written list of the concerns from him so they might be dealt with. If there is merit in the criticism correct whatever needs correction. On the other issues give a pointed response and always take a witness with you.

Give it the attention it is due; when possible move on

If you feed any animal it will grow stronger. Leadership reinforces whatever it gives its attention to. When questions arise deal with them and move on. Often one contentious person in a church becomes the focal point for every leadership conversation and meeting. I have told our board in regards to one Absalom, "We have dealt with this individual. We know he is not happy. There is probably nothing we can do to change his mind. But there are hundreds of people in this church who need and want our attention. I would consider it a favor if you would stop bringing that name up at each board meeting."

If you placed a dot on a blank 8" x 11" sheet of paper, handed it to someone and asked, "What do you see?" the normal response would be "a dot." However 99.99 percent of the paper is blank. Discipline your thoughts and conversations to remain focused on the clean sheet of paper.

When divisive behavior becomes flagrant and disruptive

At this point, the leader must insist the offender be dealt with.

- ◆ Do not go alone.

- ◆ Be prepared to document specific offenses. This means others must be willing to allow you to quote them.

- Do not begin the confrontation unless you're prepared to take it to its final conclusion. Depending on your situation, it may be the elder board, congregational meeting, or denominational office.

- Be prepared to have everything in your life brought under a microscope.

- Keep calm.

- Assure the divisive person your goal is restoration and mean it, but there will be no return to business as usual.

- Do not make threats you cannot follow through on. For example, pastors don't have authority to unilaterally pull someone's membership.

- After the confrontation keep short accounts. If a resurgence of criticism comes to your attention, deal with it immediately.

Be prepared to hear "It's everyone's right to have an opinion."

Yes, and it is all Christians' obligation to keep opinions to themselves when they disrupt the fellowship and create unrest. The Scriptures teach unity within the body and boldness outside the body. Contentious people reverse these admonitions.

Summary

Four more common characteristics of turnaround leaders have been identified. Leaders realize backtracking loses respect. They mean what they say and follow through on plans once announced, recognizing as they do so there will be no church renewal without change and change will bring opposition. They are first and foremost students of God's Word. From it comes an understanding of what actions are non-negotiable. They familiarize themselves early with the church's governing document to discover what is and what is not permissible. They constantly monitor their backing so they can move from a position of strength. They also are acquainted with Robert's Rules of Order, realizing it can be a useful tool. Losing one's temper is a luxury the turnaround leader can ill afford. He remains calm under pressure, increasing the confidence of those around him. Selection of close friends and confidants becomes a matter of extreme caution. He knows he is "always on duty." Finally, turnaround leaders do not shy away from confronting the sin of divisiveness. Its destructive practice merits whatever measures available to stop it. Like a cancer, left unchecked, it will in time prevent health. When confronting the schismatic individual, the pastor always takes along a witness and the assurance that he has the full backing of his executive board.

CHAPTER 9

Characteristics of Turnaround Leaders (continued)

#9 *Turnaround leaders possess "growth vision."*

Some pastors are content with the size, health, programs, influence, outreach, facilities, giving, and rate of progress of their church, especially if the rate of growth is upward. Eighty-five percent of America's 350,000 congregations are experiencing less than 25% decadal growth. Maintenance-oriented pastors live with this comfortably as long as the people are kind, listen attentively when they speak and offerings support their annual cost of living increases. When you visit with such pastors they appear to be wholly unconcerned with the lack of growth in their church. Their conversation centers on individual stories as opposed to the composite picture.

The heart of the growth vision

In contrast, turnaround leaders are never content unless there is hard evidence of healthy growth. Dan Spader, founder of Sonlife Ministries, suggests churches may consider themselves healthy when they achieve the 10 percent figure; that is at least one conversion per year for every 10 attenders on Sunday morning. I have found baptisms to be the preferred manner to track conversions. Baptisms (unless you practice infant baptism) are a somewhat more substantial indicator of faith than a raised hand or prayer, which are often made in a moment of crisis. Thus a church might hope for one baptism annually for every 10 attenders. If your church is averaging 100 in attendance then 10 baptisms per year would be a minimal goal for your church. 500 in attendance? The goal would be 50 or more baptisms per year.

Occasionally churches grow significantly because of transfer. A large church across town experiences a split and a group transfers to another church. Or rapid growth takes place in the community. Or a new exciting worship leader attracts people due to a superior worship experience. Or a new pastor in town is an unusually gifted pulpiteer. Turnaround leaders will gladly accept these transfers (with a smile), but none of them are content even with this pleasant trend.

A paradox of superb leadership is the responsibility to create holy dissatisfaction. Turnaround leaders do this. They are never satisfied until the lost are being won to Christ, discipled, and assimilated into their congregation in healthy numbers. This is a distinguishing and predictable characteristic of a turnaround pastor.

Please remember that we are not looking at pastors who have been used of God to build one effective ministry in their careers and have remained to see it grow into a large congregation. We are considering those uniquely gifted to move into several dying existing churches over a lifetime of service and provide the leadership necessary to resurrect them to life and spiritual vibrancy. This is a different species. Moving a church from the brink of death requires the leader to infuse large amounts of new blood while simultaneously dealing with a bad cut.

Without a passion for evangelism from the key leader, this will never happen. It does not happen solely by praying, by wishing, by luck, or waiting for fortuitous external causes. In every case a leader is present who carries the banner "Make us godly, then give us souls." This tandem desire is the deepest burden of his heart.

It is probably not too strong in this context to make passion for lost souls synonymous with "vision." There is more to the vision as we will see, but in the turnaround environment evangelism is the sina qua non of the vision. Without a burden for lost people the church will continue on its merry way to demise. Always!

Developing a unique growth vision for your congregation

During the past decade, the term "vision" has been identified as the key to all effective ministry. It is such a lofty and mystical sounding word. But what does it mean in the local church?

I appreciate Leith Anderson's practical and honest dealing with this issue in his fine book *Leadership That Works* (Minneapolis: Bethany House Publishers, 1999, p.196).

> What is the usual way to get the vision? Is it for the leader to take a week alone fasting in the desert while God implants it into the leader's head?
>
> Most visions come from a lengthy process of learning, praying, observing, brainstorming with others, trial and error, rough drafts, trial balloons, false starts, refinement, partial agreement, eventual adoption, and incremental implementation ...
>
> If the vision turns out well, they (leaders) emphasize the desert and mountaintop pieces of the story.

Building a growth vision for my church

Let's examine four essential ingredients when developing a compelling vision for a turnaround church.

1) Confidence – exuded

2) Motives – examined

3) Circumstances – evaluated

4) Wisdom – experienced

Confidence

Jesus said, "I will build my church" (Matthew 16:18). No caveats, no maybes, no sometimes. The arch enemy Satan cannot stop the steady march of progress for "the gates of hell will not prevail against it." As surely as Jehovah gave the land to Joshua saying, "Be strong and coura- geous" (Joshua 1:9), He has said to us today, "Go into all the world and preach the gospel, and I will be with you always" (Matthew 28:19-20).

God has and is building His church today

I recently spent time in China. God is building His church. Exact figures are unknown because of the large house church movement which func- tions underground. Some suggest 28,000 per day are finding Christ as Lord and Savior (Bill and Amy Stearns, *Catch the Vision 2000*, Bethany House, 1991). What astounded me was the health of the state church, the CCC. Even government officials with the Religious Affairs Bureau in Beijing admitted evangelical churches were flourishing in China. In the provinces, regional authorities, though many were self-proclaimed athe- ists, were fascinated by the growth of the Christian church in their areas. When asked if evangelism and baptisms were taking place, they smiled and said, "We invite you to go and look for yourselves."

In the Philippines the gospel continues to spread like wildfire. The CBAmerica affiliate (Conservative Baptists of the Philippines) set a goal for each church to plant two daughter churches in the last decade. In large modern buildings in major cities, in crude shacks located along jungle paths, wherever we traveled churches were being planted.

Korea may be 30 percent Christian. In the former Soviet Union, Christians now number approximately 100 million, five times more than the membership of the Communist party at its peak.

Willow Creek, in the greater Chicago area, and Saddleback, in Mission Viejo, California, are seeking solutions as they plan to soon exceed 20,000 worshippers per weekend.

A church in your town is doing superbly. They see baptisms with regu- larity, their worship center is full, and they are preparing to build. The same is happening to numerous churches in other towns surrounding you amidst all denominations. **Jesus is building His church**.

Turnaround leaders know this. The cry of their heart is, "God please use me! Wherever you take me, I crave to be an integral player in your process of building your church. Why not here Lord?" Yes, they believe it will be wherever they are.

God's Word is powerful and sufficient

Turnaround leaders are confident in the power of God's Word. They don't spend as much time defending it as using it. It is "quick and sharp and piercing." It will not return void. They expect their messages to produce results. They accept it as the final arbiter in all matters of dispute. They would rather be fired than compromise it. They do not elevate their own opinions to the status of Scripture.

A startling observation

Ready for a shocking statement? I have not discovered turnaround leaders to be more godly than other pastors! Most are quite candid in this regard. They don't necessarily pray more than other colleagues. They probably did not graduate in the top percentile of their class in seminary. They don't spend more time studying than other preachers. Nor do they fast more, memorize more, or meditate more. They are not spiritual superheroes though they strive for authenticity.

This is confusing. Some could conclude that their turnaround capabilities are thus works of the flesh and ego-drive. That, however, is not generally true. They are unusually humble in acknowledging the hand of God in their successes. They don't need their name emblazoned all over every sign, bulletin, and advertisement. The reality is they do the right things longer, with more energy, and with more focus than those who fail. They exude confidence in God's power to accomplish His great commission through them.

Motives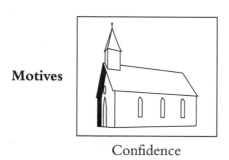

Confidence

> Now if any man builds upon the foundation with gold, silver, precious stones, wood, hay, straw, each man's work will become evident; for the day will show it, because it is to be revealed with fire; and the fire itself will test the quality of each man's work (1 Corinthians 3:13-14).

Turnaround leaders are agonizingly aware that their efforts are not to be motivated by recognition, higher pay, ego gratification, lust for power, or career advancement. These can be tempting, so quality leaders continually look deep inside themselves to clear out vestiges of motive corruption.

As they rode together in a carriage, Abraham Lincoln debated with a friend as to whether there was any such thing as an act performed with a totally "unselfish motive." Lincoln argued there was not; that every act, no matter how altruistic and selfless it appeared, had a twinge of self-gratification.

The weather outside their carriage was miserable. Rain poured down and the temperature was cold. In the courage of their conversation, Lincoln abruptly halted the carriage, and without a word jumped from the carriage. A pig was stuck in a nearby fence. Lincoln waded through the mud and freed the squealing animal.

When he returned to the carriage dripping wet his friend crowed triumphantly: "See, you have proven my point. That was a selfless act."

"No," replied Lincoln, "for if I had not done it the sound of the pig squealing would have haunted me all night."

It is difficult to accurately evaluate our own motives. The Apostle Paul admitted as much:

> I am conscious of nothing against myself, yet I am not by this acquitted; but the one who examines me is the Lord. Therefore do not go on passing judgment before the time, but wait until the Lord comes who will both bring to light the things hidden in the darkness and disclose the motives of the men's hearts; and then each man's praise will come to him from God (1 Corinthians 4:4-5).

When turnaround begins to take place, be prepared for attacks on your motives

What makes these accusations regarding your motives so agonizing is they are impossible to defend against. How can one prove what is or is not in his heart?

The greater lengths to which one goes to defend his motives the more guilty he appears. The best response is probably, "You are wrong. I am aware good deeds can be done with impure motives and so have attempted to keep short accounts with God. Since you cannot know my heart, why don't we keep our conversations focused on actions and issues. Now what is going on that you are concerned about?"

The motive attackers may be ruthless and vocal

In the midst of one heated battle for turnaround, a woman representing the pioneers in the church decided to leave with a final hurrah. Because she loved missionaries she wrote a letter to the dozens of missionary families the church supported and explained they would be moving on but would be continuing to pray for them. She then proceeded to share all the terrible things her pastor had done to the church. The letter closed with a Bible verse: "With him is only an arm of flesh, but with us is the Lord our God to help us and to fight our battles" (2 Chronicles 32:8a).

When the missionaries received the letter many of the veterans simply put it in an envelope and returned it to the pastor with a note, "We're praying for you."

This pastor stated to a close friend, "I never thought of myself as Sennacherib the Assyrian before." While admiring his sense of humor, in truth the accusation of doing ministry in the "flesh" stings more than any disagreement regarding philosophy of ministry, methodology or direction. It is impossible to defend except with the course of one's life.

What are some motive attacks you may hear?

- ◆ All he cares about is numbers.

- ◆ He doesn't care about older people.

- ◆ He only spends time with the new members.

- All he wants is a yes-board.

- He is trying to get rid of everyone who has been in the church for more than a decade.

- Everything needs to be done his way.

- Once the church grows he'll use it as a stepping-stone to something bigger.

- Pastor just wants to have a mega-church.

- He is more interested in business principles than biblical principles.

- I don't think he even prays.

- He doesn't like me because I disagree with decisions being made.

- He is not really called to ministry.

- He is more interested in attracting people than really proclaiming God's Word. That is why he doesn't preach on sin more often.

- He hides behind the pulpit. That is why he preaches on sin so much.

- Our pastor opposes programs just because they have been around a long time.

- Pastor has no heart for missions.

- Pastor is just trying to use the new music because that is what they taught him at the seminar.

- Pastor just wants a larger church so he can be paid more.

The positive side of motive questioning

If a work is to be blessed by God the motives of its leaders need to be pure. Though it hurts to hear these comments it does force the leader to take a hard honest look at why he does what he does. He can ask himself:

- Why do I want to see lost people come to Christ? Am I evangelistically minded as a lifestyle or only when it has potential for immediate impact on my local church?

- Why are numbers important? Is it sincerely because Jesus died for people and each person translates to a number? If so, do I rejoice internally when I hear of the successful growth of other churches?

- Will I be truly content if God's plan is for me to remain in this church for the remainder of my ministerial career? Or do I secretly view this as a stepping-stone to another larger church?

- Do all the creative ideas need to be my own? Or am I delighted when others have a better idea? What goes on inside of me when someone else receives praise for the growth we are enjoying? When someone else receives credit for an idea I originally suggested do I need to make sure they know it was originally my idea?

- If someone else is more ably suited to bring growth here am I willing to remove myself and allow him to do it?

- Have I on occasion used the pulpit to vent my frustrations with members' resistance? If so, was it because I was afraid to confront them one-on-one in a biblical manner?

- Is my service about me or Him?

- Am I functioning in the flesh? Is my Bible reading and prayer life what I know it ought to be?

What are my motives?

Motives 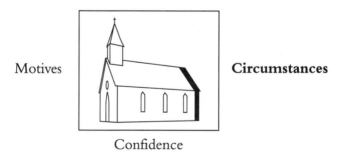 **Circumstances**

Confidence

Principle of the eclectic vision

This book is purposely void of specifics when it comes to what the church program will look like in a turnaround endeavor. The reason is that the "what" is unique to a given church situation. It is dangerous to borrow an existing model and attempt to copy it. Barna refers to this behavior as the "ministry of mimicry."

Turnaround leaders, however, *are* eclectic in their "growth vision." They read prolifically. They attend seminars and network with other effective peers incessantly, asking probing questions. They are always searching for that one golden idea which may be transferable to their needs. However they are noticeably eclectic in their visions for the church. Often what they do to succeed would be virtually impossible to reproduce elsewhere. They begin with the circumstances God handed them, become a student of their situation, and implement a course of action tailor-made to their church. They waste little energy wishing things were different. Remember the phrase "current reality"!

What works in one church may be counter productive in another

In my first two churches I personally led and trained our weekly evangelistic outreach each Monday night. I developed the material (similar to Evangelism Explosion) and wrote a nine-week discipleship follow-up program. In addition to the Monday night visitation of guests to our worship services, parents of children in our programs, and cold calling, I spent two nights per week discipling in homes. I preached Sunday morning, Sunday nights, and Wednesday nights and also taught a Sunday school class. When the churches were small this schedule impacted the church positively.

Today, I preach 42 weekends of the year, am not routinely involved on Wednesday or Sunday nights and do not teach Sunday school. A staff member oversees our weekly visitation program, promotion, and outreach activities.

The change is mostly – though not completely – due to the variation in size of the congregations. Some of the changes have more to do with the changing culture. Los Angeles is vastly different than central Pennsylvania and the Midwest, the locations of our first two pastorates. Be cautious about automatically transferring what worked for you in one church to the next. While size of the church is important (review chapter 6) it is not the only significant factor to consider.

What are some critical circumstantial ingredients other than the size of the church?

♦ How old are you? Who are you realistically going to attract most easily? We attract what we are. This does not mean a pastor in his fifties and sixties cannot attract young couples. In fact, we have a church in our hometown that has accomplished this very thing in a remarkable way. A pastor, however, does need to play to his natural strengths. What would the church programming look like if you do succeed in reaching your peer age group? Move accordingly and adjust if something else occurs.

♦ What are your strengths? A congregation gains confidence in its leader when what he proposes works! Therefore he should attempt in the beginning what has a high probability of succeeding. These initial events, programs, and concepts need not be brilliant or spectacular just accomplishable. Dying churches have lost hope! They reek with despair. The glory days have come and gone and now they are prepared to bury the corpse. The turnaround task is to restore hope. Victories, no matter how small, begin the process.

♦ What special gifts do you have? Are you capable of leading an inspiring worship service? Do so. Maybe not every week, and certainly not forever, but at first. Are you good with children's ministries? Start there. Can you invigorate a youth group? Do it. Are you a certified jock? Begin sports teams and outreach programs. Perhaps you and your wife are exceptional guides for couples. Announce a family and marriage retreat. Play to your strengths. Do you excel in Scripture memory? Introduce an inspiring and encouraging year of church-wide Scripture memory. The rule of thumb for the initial thrust of a turnaround leader is "first things first and second things not at all." The church needs wins. The pastor needs wins. Build the *esprit de corps*.

♦ What is the history of the church? One pastor told me that on his first Sunday in his new church he suggested they sing "Oh for a Thousand Tongues to Sing," commenting that that was his goal for the church. Since there was only a handful present, and the congregation had never averaged more than 75, I suspect his people viewed him more as a buffoon than a visionary leader.

Given where the church has been, what might your people reasonably buy into? Dreams are fine, but achievable goals are more inspiring. A leader who lives in the world of reality is more likely to gather followers.

A turnaround leader begins with an analysis of the church's history. As he becomes acquainted with the congregation he will hear numerous stories and anecdotes about the past. Few will be accurate and many contradictory. Some will aggrandize the past; others minimize accomplishments. History is rewritten for several reasons. Some have an agenda to keep the church small. Others wish to glorify one previous pastor over others. A few are forgetful. And most simply don't pay attention to figures.

Budgets and attendance figures never tell the whole story but they help to validate and confirm the real story of a church. To the extent records are available, chart the Sunday school and worship attendances for as far back as you can discover them. Then choose the peak attendance during the past 20 to 25 years. This will suggest a reasonable goal to work toward. Ask questions of those who were involved during the glory days of the church, such as, "Why do you think our church grew so rapidly and what was responsible for its subsequent decline?"

What is the culture? Every community has a definitive culture as does each church. The pastor must learn both. It does not mean he will necessarily choose to join the culture but he must understand it. In fact, most effective turnaround pastors make a conscious choice not to "go native." The moment we become like the people in a decaying church we lose our ability to help them rise to a new level.

There are aspects of a culture that may be adopted without hindering one's ability to lead. Other ingrown traits, habits, and patterns are directly responsible for the downward trend and must be re-engineered.

We begin by understanding culture before determining how or whether to go with it or change it. The wise pastor disciplines himself with a non-judgmental attitude. Listen, smile and commit yourself to nothing is good advice.

◆ What discernable factors contributed to the demise?

A checklist may prove helpful:

- Demographic changes in the community?

- Poor leadership?

- Strong visionary leadership without adequate administrative oversight?

- Too much gray hair?

- Inward focus on relationships without the balance of intentional evangelism?

- An ill-advised, overly aggressive building program?

- An entrenched resistance to change?

- Looking back to the glory days and attempting to repeat the methodologies of that time?

- Facility strangulation? Too small? Unwilling to expand?

- Doctrinal heresy?

- Exceptionally poor pulpit ministry?

- Lack of loving relationships within the body?

- A controlling one or two individuals?

- A dictatorial pastor?

- Pastoral leadership that felt comfortable with a smaller church?

- Deteriorating facilities?

- Declining, unsafe neighborhood?

- Inadequate assimilation procedures?

- Unwillingness of people to give financially?

- The loss of one or two major donors?

- History of short-term pastors?

- ❑ Overemphasis on one of the four major objectives: evangelism, exaltation, edification or encouragement to the exclusion of the others?

- ❑ Theological disputes?

- ❑ Moral failure of leaders?

- ❑ A Christian school sapping the church's resources and becoming the tail that wags the dog?

- ❑ A shift from a Bible teaching emphasis to a social or cause focus?

- ❑ Lack of parking?

- ❑ Ethnic groups at odds within the church?

- ❑ A large growing church very nearby?

- ❑ Open sin permitted to exist within the membership?

A thorough and honest evaluation of your church circumstances must be done before a workable growth vision is presented. Turnaround leaders have trained themselves to be far above average in seeing what most miss. Observers often believe them to be lucky. Not so; their corporate observation skills are more finely honed. This means that in time the plan which they develop will address the true needs of the church.

Summary

In this chapter we have discussed the first three of four essential ingredients when developing a growth vision for our church.

- ◆ Confidence – exuded: Yes we can!

- ◆ Motives – examined: Why do I wish this church to enjoy a turnaround?

- ◆ Circumstances – evaluated: Do I truly understand what has taken place here?

CHAPTER 10

Seeking Wisdom for the Turnaround

Wisdom

Motives 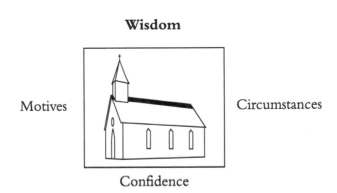 Circumstances

Confidence

The final ingredient we'll consider in the formulating of a growth vision is wisdom. Of course wisdom comes from God (James 1:5), but specifically how does He impart it? While you may hope to find it through an inner peace or special revelation, that is subjective and potentially dangerous. Certainly the prayerful and cleansed mind can be filled with the Holy Spirit's thoughts, but is this the primary means of discovering wisdom?

Proverbs provides a clue to the mechanism through which the Lord usually communicates wisdom when the writer repeatedly expresses the need for wise counsel from other people (11:14; 15:22; 24:6).

Specifically, a turnaround leader needs counsel in four major areas. It is doubtful one person will be able to provide competent counsel in all of these areas.

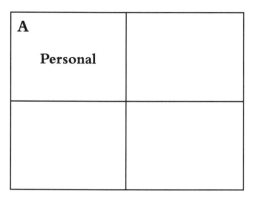

Finding Wisdom in all Areas

A. Counsel regarding who I am — Personal

Our hearts are deceitful and wicked, according to Jeremiah and "who can know it?" (7:19). That means we not only have the potential of deceiving others but worse, ourselves. We must find one or two persons who will tell us the truth about ourselves.

It's been noted that there are only two groups of people who will tell us the truth, our worst enemies and best friends. Wouldn't we prefer to hear it first from a friend?

In the process of implementing new strategies and ways of doing church, opposition will surface eventually. It is inevitable. Adversaries will spot and flag for the world your weaknesses and blind spots. As a plan of action begins to form in your mind you should approach someone whom you have known intimately for many years and who has observed your ministry. Lay out the blossoming plan and write out the role you will be called upon to play. Ask this trusted mentor, friend, or family member if he honestly believes you posses the requisite skills, personality, and courage to be successful.

The following questions cover many of the skills required by turnaround pastors. Use them as a starting point to develop a series of questions that your advisor can use to give you an honest appraisal of your skills.

- Would you review the 10 characteristics listed in chapters 7-9 of this book and evaluate me on a scale of 1-8 for each?

- After listening to tapes of my predecessor preach, in your honest opinion, do I preach appreciably better than he?

- Do people find me inspiring? If not, what do I need to change in myself to make that happen?

- In what areas do I convey confidence? Weakness?

- Are there character flaws that I need to address before heading into this plan of action?

- If you could list only one thing I do exceptionally well, what would it be? Will that be a major help in the plan of action I've outlined?

- In your opinion, what one or two things are most likely to make me lose my temper?

- Do I appear to have the internal constitution to withstand elongated criticism and alienation from a large core of my congregation?

- What is my most obvious annoying mannerism?

- Given what you know about me personally and the outline I've given you, what do you think my chances of success might be?

- What one or two things can I change in myself personally to enhance my chances of success?

- What do you perceive is my greatest area of vulnerability?

A	B
Personal	**Professional**

Finding Wisdom in all Areas

B. *Counsel regarding what I should do — Professional*

You have been brought to the church to help develop an effective course of action. It is easier for a counselor to respond to specific proposals than to help you develop one. Initially, your plan should be elastic with a number of options.

Take the embryonic strategies you have developed to a couple of trusted professionals. I am referring to someone with extensive firsthand experience in actually doing what you hope to do. Researchers, seminary professors, and consultants are all possibilities. Look for practitioners, if possible; those who have gone through a turnaround and come out the other end alive and well. Do not miss the word "trusted."

A word that I wish did not need to be said

The first choice is often the denominational executive. In most cases that is a wonderful choice. But they are people too. "Trusted" means they can be trusted not to share your conversations with the key members of your congregation. Not now, not ever. Struggling and dying churches have two common tendencies. One, they turn pastors over quickly. Two, they are often run by one or two deep pocket donors. In some cases the denominational official has long ago given up on the church. He has two hopes. First, that someday the church will deed the property to headquarters. Second, the deep pocket donors will continue to be a source of income for the denomination. Bottom line, the church and its resources are more important than the pastor du jour.

How do know if a fellow professional (clergy or denominational) is trustworthy? Easy. If he talks to you about others, he will be talking to others about you. Denominational executives understand information is power, and a few are anxious to impress everyone they talk to with how much power they have. They usually are not purposefully malicious. They fail to comprehend how sensitive some issues can be in a turnaround situation. If you sense the denominational executive has a higher loyalty to some of the influential members in your congregation than to you look elsewhere. Chances are very good the decisions and plans you'll need to implement will alienate at least some of the longtime power brokers in your congregation.

When you visit with your "trusted professional," you will be sharing your initial observations about the members, board, staff, and their spouses. Do you want these early conclusions to come back to bite you? Of course not.

Assuming your counselor has prior knowledge of the church, you may ask:

- Do you think I was foolish to take this church?

- Why?

- What do you see happening at our church in five years?

- You have now heard my plans on where I'd like to take the church. What is your evaluation?

- What pitfalls do I need to avoid?

- Based upon your knowledge of the congregation whom do you think I can trust? Whom do I need to be cautious of?

- What part of my plan do you think will encounter the greatest opposition?

- Who do you know who has faced a situation similar to our own?

- What one specific thing would you do differently than what I am proposing?

- Is there anything you feel I need to know that you haven't told me?

- If this fails would you be willing to assist me in finding another place of ministry?

A	B
Personal	Professional
C **Spiritual**	

Finding Wisdom in all Areas

C. Counsel regarding who I need to become — Spiritual

The best counselor is yourself. You know who you are better than anyone else but God. You have been indwelt with the Holy Spirit who tugs at your conscience whenever He is grieved or quenched.

The single best indicator of genuine spirituality is how often we are in the Word when we are not obligated by our ministerial occupation. Convicting? Probably. It certainly has been for me throughout periods of my life. Either the book will keep me from sin or sin will keep me from the book.

There is a plethora of books available to assist us in our spiritual walk. A couple of my favorites are Lewis Sperry Chafer's work *He That is Spiritual* (Grand Rapids: Zondervan Publishing House, 1918) and Miles J. Stanford's booklet *Principles of Spiritual Growth* (Lincoln: Back to the Bible Broadcast, 1996). What is your favorite? Read it again. You simply do not want to move ahead without the empowerment of the Spirit of God.

Many pastors point to accountability groups as a partial solution for guaranteeing ongoing spiritual authenticity. If so, fine. I have always questioned their ability to deal with the inner recesses of my soul. If I can lie to God, my wife, children, and my congregation, I will not have a great problem lying to a group of men.

If an accountability group does assist you in the quest for godliness, you probably should not find it within the congregation at the beginning of a turnaround. It is simply too risky, in my opinion. It will be years before you know who is trustworthy. Anything with potential for good has a proportionate potential for bad.

A	B
Personal	Professional
C	**D**
Spiritual	**Congregational**

Finding Wisdom in all Areas

D. Counsel regarding where we are headed and how we will get there — Church leaders

At some point in the candidating process, the pastoral search committee will ask, "What is your plan for our church if you come?"

My stock response has always been, "Beyond preaching the Word, loving the people, and attempting to win the lost to Christ I really have no plan at this time. If you call me and I feel it's the Lord's will to accept, we will need to discover the plan together sometime during the first year."

This accomplishes two things. It sends a clear message that we will have a plan and own it together, and it buys some time. A pastor-leader only has one chance to make a first impression. If the first proposals fail, it will become increasingly difficult to raise the enthusiasm level for plan two, three, or four.

In chapter 7, I laid out the gist of the annual planning meeting. Sometime within the first three to six months after arriving you can call for a planning meeting. The letter should remind the invitees of several things:

1) This is an ad hoc meeting. Some churches are paranoid of anyone having a say in the church's future except the officially elected board. Stress this is only for the purpose of analysis, discussion and recommendation.

2) You wish to hear their thoughts. All opinions and perspectives will be heard.

3) Ask them to clear their calendar of all possible conflicts. You have served notice of the meeting far enough in advance so they can do this. Tell them you believe this will be a life-changing event for the church. Raise the bar of expectation.

Why this works

There is a natural level of expectation. Most members expect the new pastor to unload all his visions to them, only to have these dreams fade away into oblivion like those of multiple pastors before him. They wait for the pronouncement through the early months. Nothing. Finally news of this letter ripples through the body. Something is happening. But not what they expected. They, or those who represent them, are being called to help formulate the vision.

Of course the official board and other decision making officers and staff are invited. But the genius of this approach is that you can invite anyone else you desire because this is an ad hoc meeting. Because you've waited several months you are beginning to surmise who the fresh, creative thinkers are. Invite them. Simply refer to them as members at large.

By the end of the meeting, a master plan has been agreed upon and one-year goals established. If run correctly, the board members have already given consent as participants in the meeting. They may not be as enthusiastic as you would like but don't let that stop the process. All you want is corporate permission to begin change. At the next official board meeting ask the board to place the decisions from the planning meeting into the minutes.

The long stagnant congregation is in for a surprise. They have held meetings before, written purpose statements, and listened to the pastor's annual pie in the sky "state of the church" message, but alas things always return to normal.

Surprise! The first day following the board's vote you begin to act on the goals that have been set. Just do it! When you're asked, "Why are you doing this?" you answer, "I must. The planning committee and board said this is what our church is doing this year."

You have received appropriate counsel from those elected by the congregation. There is nothing preventing you now from moving ahead. Just do it!

#10 *Turnaround leaders are action-oriented and bold.*

After painstaking evaluation, countless proposals, risks, calculations and assessment of personal and financial resources there comes a time to act. Acting too hastily could bring disaster. Not acting assures it.

Somewhere in the process a little voice speaks to most turnaround leaders suggesting that perhaps status quo is preferable to what charging into change might bring. Don't listen to the voice! If you take no steps toward a brighter future the church will continue its dismal descent. You will die by degrees. Surely your spirit and your career will go along with it.

If you are traveling into the Mojave Desert would you opt to have a blowout while you're at a service station or a slow leak that will leave you stranded somewhere undetermined?

You're in a declining church. The air is slowly seeping from your tires. Turnaround pastors determine to take the tires off, patch or replace them and get on down the road.

Will it be easy? No. Are you assured of success? No. Will the task challenge you to the max? Yes! But who said ministry was easy? It is, in fact, no place for the timid.

I found a quote, which also hangs in a prominent place (my office bathroom). It says, "Thank God for your difficulties. If your job was any easier any dummy could do it."

I leave with a verse to hang on to: "Have not I commanded you? Be strong and courageous! Do not tremble or be dismayed, for the Lord your God is with you wherever you go" (Joshua 1:9).

Summary

The turnaround leader considers his own age and strengths, the church history and culture in formulating plans. Finally, he is determined to act wisely, which includes seeking outside counsel. This helps him answer the questions:

- ◆ Who am I? Evaluate strengths and weaknesses. (from close friends and family)

- What can I do quickly to get off to a good start ? (professional colleagues)

- What do I need to work on spiritually? (self and God)

- Where should the church head? What is its master plan? (church leadership)

Finally, successful leaders are action-oriented.

CHAPTER 11

Why Leaders Settle for Plateau and Decline

The statistics in chapter 3 show that the overwhelming majority of churches in America are plateaued or in sharp decline. Nationwide we close seven more churches per day than we plant. This book argues that turnaround is possible with qualified leadership.

Why don't more pastors take steps to bring change within their congregations?

Frankly, a significant proportion of church leaders are content with status quo. You hear comments such as: "This is all I can handle." "Winning the lost is God's business not man's." "We are a teaching church." "We don't want to proselytize." "This is a small community and everyone already has a church home." "The mega–church down the street draws the crowds. We cannot compete." "We are landlocked. Our facility will not accommodate more people than we have now."

But what about the thousands of leaders such as yourself who sincerely desire to grow a healthy church? You agonize over the condition you see in your church. Frustration has been building over what appears to be an impossible task of instilling new hope and vision. You began seminary or Bible college with big dreams. Those dreams have not died. You're not ready to give up but are honest enough to admit there is something missing. You care enough to change whatever you can. This last chapter is for you. There are at least four identifiable factors which may prevent godly and otherwise capable leaders from enjoying the great harvest the Lord may have for them. At least one but usually several are discovered in plateaued ministries. They are not listed in order of importance as any one of these can prevent a leader from reaching his maximum effectiveness.

Skim these pages quickly. If any of the four factors hits a personal nerve, stop and reflect. The purpose here is not to add more criticism to your life, rather to offer several areas for consideration which might increase your pastoral effectiveness exponentially. You can change. Yes you can!

Factors which may prevent us from being all we can be

1. Fear of conflict

Nancy Ammerman, the director of a recent congregational study finished at Emory University, confirmed that every congregation that successfully adapted and flourished in a changing community had at least one substantial church fight. All churches who chose to avoid conflict at all costs failed to move beyond their current level. No exceptions.

Ammerman noted: "It is extremely rare in my work as a sociologist to have a one-to-one correlation" (*Net Results*, January 1996, page 26). Repeat: In this study there were no exceptions to the rule. This reality cannot be denied. Anecdotal evidence collaborates Ammerman's findings. Find a church which moved significantly beyond its long time plateau and you will discover some unhappy people.

When a significant number of new members arrive in a short period of time (probably anything greater than 15 percent of the total attendance), the potential for conflict is inevitable.

As long as these new members are content to simply sit, perform menial tasks and give, things will likely go along peaceably. But this is neither biblical, nor desirable. When the newcomers begin to offer suggestions as to how the church might be more effective in bearing fruit, the old-timers are offended. Even more significantly, when new members are placed into positions of leadership or given regular places on the platform, conflict is assured.

I actually heard one church power broker say, "If we don't do something, all these new people will be able to outvote us." Usually the fear is couched more subtly. The established members begin to express "concerns." In many churches, the issues are Pharisaic in nature. "Did you notice what they wore?" "Why don't the new members come on Sunday night?" "What was that Bible translation they read from?" "Did you know they were divorced?" "How could he be on our board? He has only been here three years. He doesn't know how we do things around here."

When these types of issues surface, the tendency of many pastors is to squelch them by being nice. I quote once again from Bill Easum's excellent article:

> I'm convinced that one of the main sins of the Church is that we have taught ourselves to be nice instead of Christian . . . One of the hallmarks of Jesus' ministry was his constant attack on the status quo. He challenged it every time he could. He even went out of His way to upset the religious bullies of his time . . . Jesus loved church leaders too much to allow them to remain such small persons . . . being nice has nothing to do with being Christian. Being nice is often nothing more than a lack of compassion for people.

If concerns and criticisms have biblical merit, of course they need to be addressed and resolved. But if they are nothing more than an attempt to force others to conform to our long-standing family rituals, that cannot be permitted to hold back the work God is desiring to do in the church.

Turnaround pastors understand that growth-resistant behavior must be checked the first time it rears its head. If longtime members are allowed to stand in the way of outreach and assimilation of new members, they will boldly continue that pattern of behavior.

When I was in grade school my parents purchased a beautiful pure-bred collie for me. I loved that dog. She was my friend. One of the ways we spoiled her was by purchasing large bones from the butcher shop. We did not know it gave her a taste for blood. She began to swing by a neighbor's chicken coop in her spare time. While we occasionally found bone fragments in the yard, we assumed they were simply dead birds she found and brought home. One day my dog didn't come home. We later found her remains lying in a field. The farmer had shot her.

When pastors permit older members to foist extra-biblical and cultural norms on new attendees, they unwittingly give the pioneers a "taste for blood." The leader who cares about the health of his congregation is willing to step in early and stop this type of growth-inhibiting behavior. It is, in fact, the most loving thing he can do.

Easum writes, "People who would rather be nice than Christian do not love enough. They do not have enough compassion. Instead they are afraid of hurting someone or of being hurt. But fear is the opposite of love. 'Perfect love casts out fear.' If we really cared about people we would not allow anyone to bully others into submission" (*NetResults*, April 1997, page 16).

A qualification given for serving as an elder is that a man must rule his own house well. Have you given that serious thought? The way a man governs his home provides the best insight as to how he will lead the church.

Would a father allow an older sibling in the home to behave in a tyrannical manner? Is the oldest child granted permission to demand the younger children cater to his every whim and preference? Of course not. Why then should pastors condone such offensive behavior in the church?

2. Lack of discipline

Professional discipline is the trademark of all successful turnaround pastors. I appreciate the work ethic given to me by my pastor-father, who taught me the value of hard work. Success seldom is the domain of the most talented or intelligent. I'm reminded often of what Howie Hendricks taught us in seminary. He said, "Every year we give awards to our most scholarly students at Dallas Seminary. Years later we are looking around trying to find out whatever happened to them." Good grades don't necessarily translate into effective pastoral ministry. In fact it is usually the B students who excel because they have a balanced life.

As I said in Chapter 3, I think it is probably reasonable for a pastor to work 55 to 70 hours per week. Most lay leaders in our churches work a minimum of 50 hours per week at their place of employment and an additional 10 to 15 hours serving in the church. Shouldn't a pastor be equally committed?

In the interest of honesty, pastors should acknowledge we have soft hours and hard hours. Not all of our work is blood sweat and tears. We are privileged with long lunches, pleasant conversations on the phone and interaction with our people, luxuries which many of our lay people do not enjoy. Fifty-five to 70 hours seems a reasonable goal.

The distinguishing feature between turnaround pastors and those who cannot develop a healthy church lies in how disciplined they are with the hours they do work.

Are you disciplined in your professional life? Perhaps the following probing questions will help you answer this accurately.

- What time do you arrive in the morning at the office? If it's later that 8:00 you may wish to re-evaluate. Of course, pastors are out at night for meetings and visitation, but so are lay leaders, and they show up for work the next morning on time.

- Do you study at home? The captain of the ship cannot navigate nor monitor the crew from shore. Once the ship is cruising this may be permissible, but in times of crises, the captain needs to be visible.

- Do you have a daily "to do" list and follow it religiously?

- Do you have a list of projects on your desk and check it daily to remind yourself of how they are progressing?

- Do you take time to plan the coming year? I have found it helpful to escape each year for a week away. During this time I can prayerfully structure a plan which maintains direction and balance for the church.

- Do you receive weekly staff reports and have a system in place for tracking attendance and giving? Do you know how this year compares with the preceding three years?

- Have you written out annual goals? What format is in place to hold you accountable for these goals?

- Does your church have a written purpose statement? If so, how many of your key leaders can tell you what that is? How often throughout the year does this purpose statement find its way into your messages, personal conversation, and written correspondence?

- What have you said "no" to this year because it did not fit your stated objectives?

- Are you habitually late to appointments, to work or with deadlines? Does your family assume you will be late to dinner?

- What new significant and meaningful ministries have you been able to implement this past year?

Leaders are out in front. Disciplined leaders always maintain control of their own calendar. One technique helpful in this regard is to work off a desk calendar as opposed to a pocket calendar. When someone requests a slice of your time, simply assure him you will go back to the office and see what your schedule is. Then, in the privacy of your office, you can see if this fits your priorities. A leader must avoid the tyranny of the urgent at all costs.

At the end of this book an addendum has been included with fifty tips for time management. These suggestions are designed for periods of life when you are buried under the workload. The goal for time management is not to be busier; rather it enables us to use the time at work in such a manner that there is free time to do the other things in life which bring fulfillment and balance.

Sadly, many leaders are perpetually playing catch up. This is often the product of an undisciplined work life. Such a pastor, let's call him pastor Robert, breezes into the office one minute before starting time, stopping to chat with others in the office. After he takes his coat off and finds a place to set down all the books he took home the night before and never had time to read, he is ready to make coffee. Ten minutes later, with coffee cup in hand, he attempts to retrieve his calendar which is somewhere in his briefcase. Eventually he reshuffles the piles of paperwork, left from when he rushed out the night before thirty minutes late for dinner. Then it's time to turn on the computer, he is not sure why, but he knows he will need it sometime later in the day. About then the phone rings. The secretary is unsure as to whether she should put the call through, but no clear instructions have been left for the morning hours so she does. Conversation ended. Now where was he? Oh yes, the computer is on, so better check e-mail. Oh, five new messages. Better read them. Yes, a message from a missionary in Zaire. No, the church doesn't support them, but the four-page form letter does tell of another coup in the works. This reminds him of the upcoming missions conference . . . add a couple of memos, another phone call . . . and the morning is gone. Exhausted from a morning of unproductivity, he rewards himself with a two-hour lunch.

Does this sound familiar? Work expands to fill the time allotted for it. Turnaround leaders budget their time more carefully than their money. The question is not so much how many hours a leader works, but what he does with the time.

3. *Inability to do personal evangelism*

In my first pastorate I was called to a small church averaging between 25 and 30 people on Sunday mornings. My wife and I were newly married. She resigned her nursing position, and I left the Teamsters job which met my needs while in Bible college, all for the joy of pastoring this struggling congregation in The Dalles, Oregon, for $600 per month.

We settled into our new apartment. The night before I was to go into the office for the first day at the church we lay in bed. Through the darkness my new bride's voice came with a question only a wife can ask. "Honey . . . can I ask you something?" "Yes, of course," I responded. "Tomorrow . . . when you go into the office . . . do you know what you're supposed to do?" "Sure," I answered with all the confidence I could muster.

The next morning I did know what to do. I rose early, ate breakfast, shaved, drove up to the church, opened the door, rearranged the couple of pieces of furniture in the tiny office and began placing all my books neatly on the book shelves. *Then* I didn't know what to do!

I had grown up in a pastor's home, but in a much larger church. In my new position there was no staff. The phone was *not* ringing. I had no administration to conduct. Just me—and Sunday still five days away. In those early days I concluded, if I did not learn how to lead people to Christ, I was in for one very lo-o-o-o-ng career.

The second week, I completed my sermon preparation and then took the few books I had in my fledgling library on personal evangelism and began to read. I will forever be indebted to men like Paul Little, James Kennedy, Robert Coleman, and others who blessed me with their insights and practical assistance through their writings.

I then drew up a crude map of our immediate neighborhood and decided to spend several afternoons per week knocking on doors. No, it was not glamorous—perhaps not even professional in the eyes of some —but it was eternally productive. Before many weeks went by we were taking the lid off the baptistry built into the platform in our auditorium.

Though the scope of our evangelistic endeavors has grown over the years, the fundamental necessity of the senior pastor demonstrating his personal concern for the reaching of lost people has never diminished. Bottom line is this: If a senior pastor is not willing and able to lead unbelievers to Christ, it is unfair to expect those who follow him to do the same.

Leaders know—people do what people see. Turnaround pastors are soul winners! The programs they use vary. Personality, philosophy, programming and preaching may change, but one factor is a given. Evangelism is priority one.

If only more leaders could understand the multiple benefits derived from the fruit of conversion in the church. There is no more central and guaranteed method of turning a church around than a passion for reaching the lost burning in the gut of the pastor.

When you visit with turnaround leaders, you will frequently see tears welling in their eyes as they speak of those with whom they share Christ. They reflect the heart of Jesus who sought to save the lost. It is contagious. Before long, the congregation comes to share this passion.

Turnaround leaders are forever telling the stories of their contacts with the unbelieving world. They tell them in personal conversation, from the pulpit, in their newsletters, at the supper table, anywhere someone will listen. What a person speaks of most naturally is the window to their heart.

4. Unwillingness to accept coaching

The term coaching is perhaps less familiar than its synonym mentoring. We have settled on coaching for several reasons. First, it assumes the one being coached is actively playing the game. Coaching also carries with it the inference that the recipient wishes to compete so as to win. Furthermore, the athletic metaphor brings to mind some of the harsh aspects of competition which translate accurately to the present-day realities of pastoring. A coach is not generally expected to be a soft gentle figure. When the church is struggling for survival, tough tactics are required. Pastoring today is not for the weak. Finally, coaches will not waste time with those unwilling to give an all-out effort.

Whenever opportunity affords itself I challenge pastors to find a coach. Surprisingly there are more pastors willing to be a coach than there are those ready to be coached.

Who needs a coach? Every pastor could benefit from having a ministerial coach. Even Michael Jordan needed a coach. As the 1998 NBA basketball season drew to a close Phil Jackson, perennial winner and coach of the Chicago Bulls, resigned. Jordan said he would not return unless Jackson was back to coach the team. Arguably the best player in the history of the sport of basketball affirmed the importance of good coaching.

There are four benefits to having a competent coach:

A) A good coach pushes us to the point of pain in practice.

"No pain, no gain" is true in most every endeavor. A price must be paid to achieve excellence. Part of the pain is saying no to what will not further the priority goals.

Each January, in the gym I frequent, a hoard of new members arrives. They have new shoes, colorful outfits and hopes for improved bodies. A leery fascination is shown for each piece of apparatus. They self-consciously experiment with the exercise equipment, whimsically hoping to find something which will magically produce the abs, thighs, biceps and quads longed for—but without too much effort. Of course no such equipment has yet been manufactured.

No pain, no gain. In fact physical development is not as much about exercise as it is life-style. Positive change takes repetitive effort. Not hours, but days, weeks and years of exhausting effort.

A weightlifter understands the necessity of achieving the "burn." When sufficient weight or reps have been performed to release the lactic acid, benefit will be realized. But this requires some discomfort and discipline. Desired results come over time. Gratification must be deferred.

This is where the coach comes in. He lays out a custom exercise routine for each athlete. He watches carefully to assure no damage is done in the developmental process and provides reassurance that "in time" the goal can be accomplished. But a good coach never permits those on his team to become lazy. Day after day and month after month he assesses, modifies, evaluates and encourages the training process, always pushing his players just a little further than they feel they can go.

In time a champion is made. He knows what it takes, because he himself has experienced the challenge.

B) A good coach helps set realistic goals.

In track and field athletes speak of their "p.r." That is their personal record for an event. Whether they had a good meet or a poor one is assessed more by how they compared to their p.r. than where they finished in the race. The p.r. serves to monitor progress but also helps them remain realistic about their capabilities and circumstances. The goal is not necessarily to win, but to steadily improve.

Turnaround pastors understand this intuitively. They are not overly consumed or preoccupied with what is happening down the street or by what the mega-churches are accomplishing. They are, however, obsessively interested in how the church they are in is doing relative to its own p.r. The goal is to bear fruit where God has called them. What they wish to know is how they can be more effective in their given circumstance than they were last week or last year.

A gifted pastor-coach will be helpful in establishing attainable goals. Unrealistic goals are demoralizing. A good coach will never tell those he works with what they want to hear simply to make them feel good. The integrity of coaching is at stake.

A number of years ago I served a church in a small town in Lewistown, Pennsylvania. We had 35 off-street parking spaces. By hard work on the part of the people and God's grace, the church experienced significant growth. In a couple of years we completed a building expansion. But at this point I could not for all my efforts figure out how to move this church beyond where we were due to facility limitations. We tried park and ride, but it didn't work, so I called Bob Humphrey, a church growth consultant, to come and observe our situation and then offer his insights.

Bob spent an entire weekend with us. As he left he said, "Gene, usually I go back to the office following an evaluation, and fill pages with recommendations. But in this case, I think you've been fortunate to take it to this level."

This was not what I wanted to hear, but it was what I needed to hear. My goals were not realistic. That church site did not lend itself to achieving what I hoped for. We either needed to move to another site or accept our limitations. Helping us accept limitations is a benefit of wise coaching.

C) *A good coach walks us through times of injury and setback.*

Sooner or later every competitor will be hurt. It comes with playing the game. Whether due to carelessness, the heat of the battle or unfair play, it will happen. In fact, it seems injury often occurs at the point of maximum performance. I know of no man in ministry who has not been hurt. Recovering is not pleasant. Should we play hurt? Or is it expedient to take time off? When making this decision, the presence of someone with perspective is essential. The wrong call may set us on the sideline permanently.

When injured, the competitor is not in the frame of mind to make calls concerning the best course of action. Due to the nature of the pastorate, frequently the cause of injury is within our own church. Whom does the leader turn to? If a trusting relationship has been developed with a mentor-coach he can help the pastor with a program for recovery.

D) *A good coach helps us finish well.*

Finishing strong is the hope of all leaders. Not only does it please the Lord who called us, it determines our legacy. How an athlete competes is mostly forgotten. How he finishes is remembered forever.

Do we have several more years of effective service? Am I slowing down and should I get out of the way and turn over my place to younger and stronger players? Am I still helping the team or have I become a drain? These are issues the coach can see more clearly than a player in the midst of the skirmish.

While competing, we also fail to see habits and techniques which deplete our energies and hinder maximum performance. We may be our own worst enemies and not realize it. The coach serves as an ally and watches for our best interests.

Turnaround pastors are hungry for coaching. But as mentioned earlier, many pastors seem unwilling to seek out a coach to enhance their efforts. As the benefits are apparent, one may ask why?

Perhaps pride plays a part. Most leaders are seminary trained. To ask another to serve as their coach is an admission they need help. Church leaders are used to giving answers, not asking questions. Pastors find it more natural to talk than to listen.

And, furthermore, many are so busy they do not think they have time for yet one more relationship. Perhaps there is an element of fear. Will their weaknesses be discovered? What if suggestions are made that they are incapable of implementing?

If a pastor desires to find a coach, a few simple suggestions may help. First, select someone you have observed sufficiently to be confident that his general approach to ministry mirrors your own. Second, find someone you enjoy being with. Third, find someone whose church is not more than twice the size of your own. Fourth, look for a coach who is close enough that you can meet face to face with some regularity. Fifth, when you are with him, spend much time listening. Go to the meetings with a list of specific questions to show you value his time. Sixth, follow his advice unless there are significant reasons for not doing so.

Summary

Encouragement has been given to take a careful look in the mirror. Have you hesitated to do what you know needs to be done because of fear of conflict? Is your personal life disciplined in such a manner to permit you to accomplish all you want to do?

Are you satisfied with the results of your personal evangelism? If all your people followed your lead would there be a steady flow of new believers in your church? Is there anyone you know who might serve as a coach for you?

Time Management

Psalm 90:12:   *"So teach us to number our days . . ."*

Luke 19:11-27:   *The parable of the "Pounds." The master left some commodity with each of the servants. They each had the same amount. Each was called to account for what they achieved with their pounds upon His return.*

It is helpful to think of our activities as falling into two categories:

    a. <u>Non-discretionary</u>: All we can do is manage these matters in such a way as to have more time for discretionary involvement.

    b. <u>Discretionary</u>: The things we choose to do based upon visions, values and purposes.

Our goal is **NOT** to become busier— but rather to become more effective in managing our lives so as to allow more time for:

    a. relaxation

    b. family time

    c. being with friends

    d. recreation

    e. tackling new challenges and dreams

Time cannot be stopped, saved, traded, or slowed. Our choice is whether we waste it, spend it, or invest it. The real issue in the tips we share under the heading of "time management" is technically "self-management" or "self-discipline."

The following list of "self-discipline" tips is not intended to be a "life-style," but rather *a game plan for those segments of life when one feels overwhelmed with too much to do* and not sufficient time to accomplish all the demands.

The list is not arranged in any particular order. Find the handful of suggestions which fit your situation and use them. The time you find available should not be used for more work, but rather be considered a reward for your self-discipline.

Fifty Self-Discipline Tips

1. Just say **NO**.

2. Use a stand-up desk. This is especially helpful when sorting mail, reading memos, articles, and studying.

3. Hold stand-up meetings. People will stick with the focus of the meeting if not allowed to sit.

4. If your office has an open door, remove all chairs from around your desk. When people come in the clear message is that this is not the place to loiter. The DMV understands this dynamic.

5. Stay out of sight. Use the back door when possible. This prevents you from appearing rude.

6. Use to-do lists religiously.

   QUOTE: A commitment unwritten is nothing more than a nice intention.

7. Use a time analysis sheet for a week. Compare (in fifteen minute blocks) what you planned to do versus what you actually did. Are there patterns?

8. Work off a desk calendar.
   a. This helps you avoid the pressure of having people looking over your shoulder while you are checking your calendar.

   b. This helps you avoid making priority decisions on the spot.

   c. You keep all the details of your schedule in one place.

9. Establish and review your life-priorities.

   QUOTE: If I don't know my priorities, everybody I meet will set them for me.

10. Have several different day-planning sheets. Familiarity breeds contempt.

11. When you suddenly remember something you've forgotten at night, get up and write it down. Do the same during the waking hours while at home. Have a designated spot for notes you make to yourself.

12. Habitually carry a stash of 3 x 5 cards or post-its.

13. Close your door. The single most effective time saver.

14. Do tasks which require creativity in your peak times.
    "Know thyself"

15. Do mundane but necessary tasks in your down time.

16. Exercise regularly.

    QUOTE: When I'm really busy I just cannot afford to neglect prayer, exercise, and Bible reading.

17. Handle (most) paper only once!

    a. We usually don't do this because we are afraid to make decisions.

    QUOTE: Most of the great challenges of our lives are simply decisions we really don't want to make.

    b. This is the fundamental principle which leads to a clear desk.

18. Develop a habit of punctuality.
    QUOTE: If you're on time . . . you're late.

19. Do two things at once. Example:
    - Drive and listen to tapes.
    - Carry cards for memory work while waiting.
    - Always carry reading material to read while waiting.
    - Exercise while waiting.
    - Work while on "hold" by using speaker phone.

20. Sleep well!

    QUOTE: Weariness makes cowards out of all of us . . . and cowards seldom make bold decisions.

21. Think of your week in twenty-one blocks of time. After you have nailed your priorities, block them off first! Push yourself to complete all work by self-imposed deadlines.

    QUOTE: Work will always expand to fill the time allotted for it.

22. Avoid events and invitations which only boost your ego.

23. When possible double your work results. Use what you do in multiple ways.

24. Become a filer, not a piler.

25. Leave your work space clean each night. The only piece of paper which should be visible when you arrive is your daily to-do list and emergency post-its.

26. Take one-a-day vitamins. Sickness lessens productivity and usually indicates I am not handling stress well.

27. Be prepared for personal appointments and phone appointments.

28. When the purpose of a visit is accomplished, end it. Remember the 80/20 rule: 20% of the time is used dealing with the business at hand. 80% of the time is spent to "be liked."

29. Do what you dislike doing first, when possible. Schedule a reward at the end.

30. The most difficult part of most tasks is beginning.

31. The goal of a to-do list is not to have a long list, but to cross things off in proper order.

32. Don't read the whole book— find the meat, and put the book away for another time. Remember the 80% rule applies to books too. 20% of the book has 80% of the content.

33. When you're very busy, avoid new things. Stick with routines. This requires less emotional energy.

34. Do first things first and second things not at all.

35. Avoid pleasure reading (newspapers, magazines).

36. Keep business breakfasts and lunches to a minimum. Most of them are simply to "be liked."

37. Communicate by FAX and e-mail. Excellent medium for relaying facts, but not for building relationships.

38. Return phone calls in one segment. Remember, this is for their convenience, not yours. Leave messages which answer their questions on the recorder.

39. When on the phone, deal with the business and hang up.

40. If possible, do correspondence with dictation.

41. Meet in their office. This means you can leave when the purpose of the meeting has been fulfilled.

42. Ask them to drive to meet you.

43. Schedule back-to-back appointments. This forces closure.

    "I really hate to be rude to George who is waiting to see me. I'm sure you understand."

44. Keep a time log for one week. Compare what you planned to do with what actually took place. Are there patterns?

45. Scrutinize on-going commitments harder than one-time commitments.

46. Screen all calls (secretary, family, answering machine).

47. Do annual planning.

48. Do your most bothersome tasks first. Get rid of the distraction.

49. Delegate:

    a. low priority items which won't have much impact.

    b. to someone who can do it 80% as well as you. Those people are easier to find and you won't be threatened.

50. Avoid television like the plague!

Other Exciting Products from ChurchSmart Resources

Natural Church Development

By Christian Schwarz

In an attempt to put denominational and cultural distinctives aside, the author has researched 1000 churches in 32 countries to determine the quality characteristics that growing, healthy churches share. Schwarz's research indicates that quality churches score high in eight quality characteristics, but will only grow to the level that their minimum factor (or lowest of these eight characteristics) will allow them. This book is a must read!

ChurchSmart price $19.95

Raising Leaders for the Harvest

By Robert Logan & Neil Cole

Raising Leaders for the Harvest introduces the concept of Leadership Farm Systems, an organic process of leadership development which results in natural and spontaneous multiplication of disciples, groups, ministries and churches. This resource kit includes six audio cassettes and an action planning guide with worksheets. Discover how to raise leaders in your church for the harvest in your community!

ChurchSmart price $60.00

Focused Living Resource Kit

By Terry Walling

Focused Living is a personal development process designed to help believers bring strategic focus to their life and ministry. Focus is obtained by examining their past (Perspective — Personal Time-Line), clarifying their future (Focus — Personal Mission Statement) and identifying resources that will facilitate future growth and effectiveness (Mentoring — Personal Mentors). This resource includes six audio cassettes, three self-discovery workbooks and a leader's guide.

ChurchSmart price $60.00